The Cardiff Five

Innocent Beyond Any Doubt

Satish Sekar

With a Foreword by Michael Mansfield QC

WATERSIDE PRESS

CONTENTS

Acknowledgements	viii
The Author	ix
The Author of the Foreword	xi
Foreword	xiii
Dedication	xix

Introduction 29
    The End of the Beginning 29
    A Notorious Miscarriage of Justice 30
    A Pattern of Concern 30
    The Unit. 32
    Tariff Outrage 35

1. Pressure — A Force to be Reckoned With. 37
    A Daunting Task. 37
    The Precedent 38
    The Transition to PACE 39
    The Post-PACE Act Cases 41
    Cranking up the Pressure. 42

2. Advances in Forensic Science 45
    A Substantial Clue — Blood Grouping 45
    DNA 47
    Advances in DNA-testing Systems. 49
    Reopened. 50
    The Prediction 51
    The Prediction Comes True. 52
    Appendix to Chapter 2 54

3. The Unit: Unsolved and Unresolved Homicides 57
    Cold Cases. 57

The Cardiff Five

Innocent Beyond Any Doubt

Satish Sekar

The Cardiff Five
Innocent Beyond Any Doubt
Satish Sekar

Published 2012 by
Waterside Press Ltd
Sherfield Gables
Sherfield on Loddon
Hook, Hampshire
United Kingdom RG27 0JG

Telephone +44(0)1256 882250
E-mail enquiries@watersidepress.co.uk
Online catalogue WatersidePress.co.uk

ISBN 978-1-904380-76-4 (Paperback)   **ISBN** 978-908162-11-3 (e-book)

Cataloguing-In-Publication Data A catalogue record for this book can be obtained on request from the British Library.

Cover design © 2012 Waterside Press. Design by www.gibgob.com

UK distributor Gardners Books, 1 Whittle Drive, Eastbourne, East Sussex, BN23 6QH. Tel: +44 (0)1323 521777; sales@gardners.com; www.gardners.com

North American distributor International Specialized Book Services (ISBS), 920 NE 58th Ave, Suite 300, Portland, Oregon, 97213, USA. Tel: 1 800 944 6190 Fax: 1 503 280 8832; orders@isbs.com; www.isbs.com

Printed by MPG-Biddles Ltd, Bodmin and Kings Lynn.

e-book *The Cardiff Five: Innocent Beyond Any Doubt* is available as an ebook and also to subscribers of Myilibrary and Dawsonera (for ISBN see above).

Why Bother? 58
The Quest for Vindication. 59
Making History. 60
Further Resolution. 63
The Pioneering Unit 64

4. The Review Process 67
The Major Crimes Review Unit 67
Hacking and LAGs. 68
Warts and All 71

5. Committed — The Investigation After Hacking 73
Broken Promises 73
Regaining Trust. 75
Phase Two 76

6. The Scientific Evidence. 81
An Integrated Approach 81
Independence and Verification 82
DNA 83
Closing in on the Killer. 86
Proved Innocent. 87

7. Identifying the Killer and the Implications 89
The Sweep 89
Inspired 90
The Case for a Complete DNA Database 92
The Identification of Cellophane Man and its Implications 94

8. The Arrest and Aftermath 97
Unmasked 97
Too Easy 98
Arrest and Aftermath 100

9. Guilty — History is Made 103
    Remand 103
    Guilty 104
    Harrington's Case 106
    Gafoor Responds 106
    The Aftermath 109

10. Characteristics of a Killer 113
    Error of Judgement 113
    Professor Canter's Offender Profile of Lynette White's Killer 116
    Another Interpretation 117
    Accountability 120

11. Lessons — Profiling Gafoor 123
    A Pitiless Coward 123
    Failing to Take Responsibility 126
    Unpredictable 127
    The Guilty Secret 130
    A Frighteningly Normal but Unusual Killer 131
    Under Fire 131
    Behavioural Investigative Advice 133

12. Tariffs — Protecting the Guilty 135
    The Final Insult 135
    The Home Secretary Loses the Power to set Tariffs 136
    Tying the Hands of the Judges 137
    Gafoor's Tariff 138
    Sadism 142
    An Inappropriate System 145
    Preventing Miscarriages of Justice 147
    The Most Important Factor 151

13. The Power of Vindication 153
    A Potent Weapon for the Innocent 153
    End of An Era 154

Bullying of Children 156
The Presumption of Guilt 157
A Change is Gonna Come 159
Posthumous Relief. 161
A Failure 164
Travesty 165
The Lessons 167

Conclusion   **169**
Vindication of the Cardiff Five 169
Justice and Reconciliation 170
A Need for a Fully Independent Judicial Inquiry 171
And What of the Collapsed Trial?. 179

Appendix 1 — Judicial Murders in Cardiff   **181**
Vindication 181
A Major Hitch. 184

Appendix 2 — Some Further Injustices   **189**

Some Frequent Abbreviations   **195**

Index   **197**

ACKNOWLEDGEMENTS

Without the unseen contributions of many people this book could not have been written, especially Ashley Wheeler, whose editing skills made the first drafts readable. Bryan Gibson of Waterside Press provided invaluable support and interest from an early stage, which is greatly appreciated.

The support and contributions of my mother, Saraswathi Sekar, brother, Chandra Sekar, sister-in-law, Aine Kaye Sekar (and niece, Sylvie), Dr. Anil Aggrawal, Roger Backhouse QC, Stuart Hutton, Ian Moore, Polly Glynn, Mia Hakl-Law, Martin Parker, David Burns, Edward FitzGerald QC, Duncan Campbell, Mags Gavan, Angela Grobben, Peter Ward Howlett, Michael Mansfield QC, Mark Metcalf, Alun Michael MP, Derek Miller, Bob Parsons, (the late) Steve Peckham, John Actie, Malik Abdullahi, Lloyd Paris, Rachid Abdullahi, Alex Waite, Gemma Waite, Leanne Waite, Joseph Harris, Carly Harris, Stephen Miller, Tony Paris, Daryl Clemens, Richard Eikelenboom, Nat Cary, Andrew Rennison, Paul Wood, Bob Woffinden, Richard Adams, Steven Bird, Belinda Holden, Letlapa Mphahlele, Nogah Ofer, Matthew Gold, Leon Mann, Gary Mills, Tony Poole, Michael O'Brien, Desmond Hughes, Pamela McGeoch, Joseph Vonley, Connie O'Callaghan and Brian Moore were essential to the whole process of research, writing and development of the book. Their assistance will never be forgotten.

Thanks are also due to various press officers, who had to field my demands for information and insistence that their organizations take responsibility for the role they played. I make no apology for that. These lessons must be learned and repetition of errors avoided.

Others such as Dave Barclay, John Little, Natalie Walker and Claire O'Brien helped greatly as well. Many people too numerous to mention by name contributed to the writing of this book as well. They all have my gratitude.

Satish Sekar
March 2012

THE AUTHOR

Satish Sekar is a freelance journalist and researcher. His work includes that for the feature film "In the Name of the Father" and TV and radio programmes such as Panorama, Trial and Error, Law in Action, Today and Channel 4 News. He has written for the *Guardian, Independent, Daily Telegraph* and other newspapers including *Private Eye*.

In 1998, his book, *Fitted In: The Cardiff Three and the Lynette White Inquiry* was published by the Fitted-In-Project, a justice organization, of which he is the founding director.[1] Soon afterwards, the case was actively re-opened by a new unit set up to examine unsolved and unresolved homicides leading, in 2003, to the real killer pleading guilty to Lynette White's murder, the first time in British history that people originally convicted were vindicated by the conviction of the person truly guilty of murder in the DNA age.

A consultant on forensic issues, Satish Sekar has been involved in various high profile issues, including in relation to police reform, police complaints, DNA-testing and related databases.

---

1. See www.fittedin.org

THE AUTHOR OF THE FOREWORD

Michael Mansfield QC is one of the UK's foremost lawyers, known for his willingness to challenge improper uses of the law, power and authority. He has appeared in many of the most famous and controversial cases of the modern era and at major public and judicial inquiries, including in relation to Bloody Sunday, the shooting of Jean Charles de Menezes, the death of HRH Diana, Princess of Wales (for Mohamed al-Fayed) and the murder of Stephen Lawrence (for his family). He has also represented clients as diverse as the Angry Brigade, James Hanratty (posthumously), Arthur Scargill (and the Orgreave Coking Plant miners), the Price Sisters, Barry George, Angela Cannings, Kenneth Noye and Michael Barrymore. His book, *Memoirs of a Radical Lawyer,* was published by Bloomsbury in 2009.

FOREWORD

This is one of the most important books ever written about criminal justice.

It would be easy to confine my remarks to the Cardiff Five case but this would be a disservice to the thrust of this narrative as well as its author. If anyone wants to know what has been going on, and going wrong, over the past half-a-century spanning my entire professional career, here it is. Written with spell-binding passion alongside meticulous research and observation, Satish Sekar has accomplished what few others have achieved. It is redolent of those magnificent French films starring Yves Montand where one man takes on the state in the pursuit of truth and justice—and succeeds.

What becomes glaringly apparent is that this no isolated case. It has become exceptional because of the motivating force exerted by Satish. Unhappily, it is one of many in South Wales and epitomises systemic failure. Most of the others, as well as the Cardiff Five case, are familiar to me because of my involvement in their appeals.

Moreover, such cases reflect an even greater malaise which has infected other police areas throughout the United Kingdom. The best known was the West Midlands Crime Squad which had to be disbanded. Another was exposed during the Macpherson Inquiry into the handling of the Stephen Lawrence murder by the Metropolitan Police Service in London—a matter which is yet to come to a final resolution following further revelations about potential corruption.

What marks out the Cardiff Five case is the tortuous route it has followed right up to the present. More so than the Guildford Four, the Birmingham Six, the Tottenham Three and the Bridgewater Four. But like those cases it demonstrates the criminal justice system's singular inability and seeming unwillingness to identify miscarriages at an early stage during investigation and trial and then to minimise the risk of repetition: a point which becomes searingly poignant given the way in which a coach and horses was driven through the protections contained in the Police and Criminal Evidence Act 1984 within a matter of three to four years of their passage through Parliament. The Court of Appeal in the judgement of Lord Chief Justice Taylor expressed its condemnation of what happened: 'Short of physical violence, it is hard to conceive of a more hostile and intimidating approach by officers to a suspect'. The court never wanted to see such behaviour again.

Stephen Miller whom I had represented on the Cardiff appeal in 1992 had been subjected to a course of patently oppressive questioning. This took place over five days, 13 hours and was contained on 19 tapes. He was bullied with hectoring and demeaning questions until his insistent denials of involvement were worn down to submissive "confessions". The recordings have left an indelible impression on my memory. At the time I almost felt I had been in the room as it happened, because I took the trouble to count how many times Miller protested his innocence — over 300. I also remember clearly the horrified faces sitting in silence at the Court of Appeal as the tapes were played. Their lordships could hardly believe their ears. As a result, that court recommended that copies be sent to the Director of Public Prosecutions and the Chair of the Royal Commission on Criminal Justice. I have also used them in talks I have presented to audiences at police conferences to illustrate the risks. The first time I did so was at Hendon Police College just after Paul Condon had taken up office as Metropolitan Police Commissioner, and the tape was silent. 'Wiped', I suggested, but no, just a fault on the line!

What shocked everyone was not only the techniques employed but also the fact that the officers were brazen enough to carry on despite contemporaneous recording of police interviews. So what went on before this measure was instituted can be readily imagined. It illustrates just how ingrained malpractice had become. The same may be said of the numerous recent examples of racism that have been caught on camera and by other means within the Met. Presently there are seven police officers facing charges out of a total of 20 under investigation. Primitive and insidious "canteen culture" has yet to be tackled effectively at the heart of policing at every level.

The police are not the only constituent element. The obvious oppressive behaviour was unchallenged by a silent solicitor who sat through the whole exercise. The prosecuting authority who had oversight prior to trial failed to stop the proceedings, or at the very least raise concerns with the courts. Three courts failed to halt the process. Committing magistrates and two trial judges were not moved to intervene. If this veritable panoply of legal expertise were so faltering in the wake of clear guidelines, we have to ask whether things have changed.

This is undoubtedly so with regard to confession evidence despite relentless efforts by successive governments to extend the period of detention without charge. But the same cannot be said about non-disclosure which has reverted to the pre-Judith Ward position. That miscarriage changed the face of the procedures necessary to ensure a fair trial. Another instance where I watched the incredulity displayed by the Court of Appeal judges confronted by flagrant malpractice across the board by all participants from police to scientists to lawyers. Regrettably, since then there has been a palpable reluctance to adhere to full disclosure which has contributed to another wrongful conviction of a young man, Sam Hallam, for a murder he persistently denied over the course of eight years which was quashed on the 18th of May 2012.

One of the worst examples concerns the convictions of Sean Hodgson for murder and rape. These were overturned on appeal in 2009 after exhibits previously claimed by police to have been destroyed came to light and provided DNA evidence which exculpated Sean after 27 years. Initially, there had also been non-disclosure of materials relating to a number of other suspects which cast doubt on Sean's complicity.

There are other areas, particularly forensic science and covertly obtained materials where dangers remain over insufficient quality control and non-disclosure. These risks are exacerbated by short-sighted draconian cuts to resources (closure of Forensic Science Service labs) and to legal aid. This was the problem in the first place when trying to undo a miscarriage. It required the good offices of investigative journalists on Rough Justice, World in Action and Trial and Error to invest time and money. Satish has done the same for longer on a shoestring, against greater odds and almost as a one man band.

In contrast, the state has devoted a sum in the region of £10 million to convicting the wrong people, and now an estimated £30 million on a failed prosecution against those alleged to have been complicit in the wrongful accusations and convictions. This is the latest development in this long-running saga that almost beggars belief. Midway through a trial of eight police officers, all retired, and two civilians the court was informed that copies of certain documents required by the defence were believed to have been destroyed. No sooner had the trial been stopped and the defendant's acquitted by the judge in December 2011 than the said documents were miraculously discovered to be alive and kicking, still in their original containers. Quite how this was allowed to occur without due diligence and enquiry remains to be investigated by the Director of Public Prosecutions. The matter is also being investigated by the Independent Police Complaints Commission. The system, it has to be said, has rarely delivered accountability in instances of this kind.

Responsibility in another sense was however accomplished. The real killer, Jeffrey Gafoor, was traced through DNA. A first in the history of miscarriages of justice. Although even here there is a real question over the appropriate tariff. Additionally three witnesses who had perjured themselves following the kind of pressure applied to Stephen Miller were also convicted. The pursuit of others was an imperative consequence of the definitive conviction of the killer: an example of true vindication for the five.

Nevertheless, the overall picture is an astonishing patchwork of injustice with many victims including the original one Lynette White. To all of them is owed a basic debt of explanation for bungling on such a grand scale. Only a Public Judicial Inquiry with powers of compulsion can begin the process of restoring public confidence by identifying the areas of default, those responsible and the type of remedial independent supervision required. In the style of the Leveson Inquiry (into the role of the press and police in the phone-hacking scandal) there has to be transparency and public scrutiny.

Questions asked behind closed doors by internal reviews are self-serving and left to collect the dust of darkness.

Whatever happens you can be sure Satish will be there airing the public conscience. Having opened Pandora's Box there will be no closure until the Angel of Hope rises up as Greek mythology would have it.

Michael Mansfield QC
May 2012

❝ Satish Sekar has been assiduous in following the events surrounding the murder of Lynette White in Cardiff in 1988. From the beginning he questioned the techniques that were used and decisions of the authorities in regard to this case and many of his views — which appeared marginal at the time — turned out to be accurate or close to the truth in a way that has certainly helped the cause of justice and investigation. As the local MP I came to respect and admire his thoroughness and persistence and he also won the respect of senior police officers and others with a knowledge both of this individual case and the processes of criminal investigation whether in regard to the use of forensic evidence or in setting the criminal investigation process in the context of the individual experiences of those who were drawn into the courtroom events that followed. His contribution has been enormous.

There remain several aspects of other unfinished business including the way in which we deal with those who are the victims of a miscarriage of justice after they have been cleared and released. Satish is right to continue to ask questions both in respect of the workings of the criminal justice system and the policies that are pursued in a society that seeks to be governed by the Rule of Law **❞**

The Rt Hon Alun Michael JP, MP is the the Member of Parliament for Cardiff South and Penarth and a former Cabinet Minister as well as having been the inaugural First Minister of the National Assembly for Wales.

❝ It was mainly through the exposure of the appalling miscarriages of justice that had taken place in the seventies, such as those involving the Birmingham Six, the Guildford Four, the Maguire Seven and Judith Ward, that the British public first became properly alerted to the sheer scale of the scandal. As more and more victims of faulty decisions or deliberate malpractice emerged blinking into the sunlight outside the Royal Courts of Justice on the Strand after a successful appeal, it became clear that these were not isolated errors but that there was a grave problem at the heart of the criminal legal system.

The case of the Cardiff Three, as it is best known, was a miscarriage of justice written in the starkest language. This was the story of three young men convicted of the 1988 murder of Lynette White in Cardiff who were freed on appeal in 1992. It is of particular significance because the real perpetrator of the murder, Jeffrey Gafoor, was finally traced through developments in DNA and, after attempting suicide, confessed to his crime, a crime made worse by the fact that he had allowed others to, as it were, serve his sentence for him. Such vindication, as Satish Sekar explains in this book, is rare. More often, a shadow of suspicion lurks over the innocent man or woman, with unsubtle hints that some of them have "got away with murder".

The Cardiff Three—sometimes called the Cardiff Five, because five men were arrested and charged and initially held in prison, although only three were convicted—was and will remain one of the most crucial cases in the history of criminal justice in the United Kingdom and is worthy of detailed examination: not only for what went wrong at the time but for the many other issues it has thrown up in its wake.

No-one is better suited to the task of explaining and unravelling the complexities of the story than Satish whose pioneering work has played a large part in our understanding of the murder and its ramifications. He has ploughed an often lonely furrow in pursuit of the story long after it had slipped from the front pages of the national press. Investigating such cases is a time-consuming and sometimes dangerous occupation and, as the demand of instant news and information has increased, it has become harder and harder for such stories to receive the attention they deserve.

The literature is a distinguished one, from Ludovic Kennedy's *Ten Rillington Place* to Paul Foot's *Murder at the Farm: Who Killed Carl Bridgewater?* and Bob Woffinden's magisterial *Miscarriages of Justice*. It is good that Satish Sekar can now add a new work to the genre **"**

Duncan Campbell is a freelance journalist who served as a senior correspondent for the *Guardian* from 1987 until 2010. He was its one time Los Angeles and previously their crime correspondent. He is the author of several books

❝ The Lynette White murder case, with its long-drawn-out repercussions, has now become one of the most important in the entire history of British criminal justice.

This is entirely because of the tireless work and extraordinary insight of Satish Sekar, who has fought for many years to achieve justice for all concerned **❞**

Bob Woffinden is an investigative journalist specialising in examining miscarriages of justice. He has written and broadcast about many important cases stretching back over a period of 30 years, including those of James Hanratty, Sion Jenkins, Jeremy Bamber and Barry George. He has written for various leading newspapers as well as the nationwide prison newspaper *Inside Time* and his books include *Miscarriages of Justice, Hanratty: The Final Verdict* and *The Murder of Billy-Jo*.

❝ At a time of continued and savage cuts in the provision of legal aid, this book acts as a reminder as to what happens when justice miscarries. This is the story of one of the most notorious miscarriages of justice in British history told by Satish Sekar, whose unremitting efforts helped lead to the vindication of the Cardiff Five. They always were innocent, but their freedom was not enough. The memory of Lynette White and her family deserved justice too and that required the conviction of the real killer, Jeffrey Gafoor.

This book shows how even a very difficult case can be solved if there is the will to investigate it thoroughly. It details how an awful miscarriage of justice was finally corrected by the conviction of the real killer. Satish's work was pivotal to achieving this, and he is keen to continue the fight to ensure that the lessons of an extraordinary case are properly learned.

However, it is inevitable that miscarriages will continue while the government cuts legal aid to the bone, making it harder for lawyers to present a thoroughly prepared defence at trial and even harder to rectify such miscarriages afterwards.

Justice cannot be achieved on the cheap. Miscarriages of justice like this devastate the lives of all who are touched by them and those affected often find that no compensation is available even when the conviction is overturned. I hope that this book will bring some of these issues some overdue public attention **❞**

Steven Bird is founding partner of Birds Solicitors, Wandsworth. Specialising in serious crime and miscarriages of justice, he has acted in some of the most high profile criminal cases. One of the UK's top ranked solicitors according to Chambers UK, he is Treasurer of the Criminal Appeals Lawyers' Association (CALA) and co-author of the *Police Station Advisers Index* (with Brian Spiro) (fourth edn. 2010, Thomson Sweet & Maxwell).

ff This is one of the most important books to have been written in the last decade on miscarriages of justice and everyone should read it. Satish Sekar has been one of the most dedicated opponents of miscarriages of justice for many years. His work has been invaluable. His persistence has also ensured that these issues have remained within the public eye. He has constantly supported those whose lives have been turned upside down by false accusations and wrongful imprisonment and his constant fight for justice has led to some very important questions being asked and issues highlighted.

Without his pioneering work to vindicate the Cardiff Five these issues would never have made it into the newspapers or into the courts.

If it had not been for Satish and his dedication to one of the most high profile miscarriages of justice in British history, the Cardiff Five case, those who were involved would probably not have been challenged and the real killer of Lynette White never brought to justice **JJ**

Mags Gavan is Chief Executive Officer of Red Rebel Films. She has a distinguished background in current affairs and documentary-making and formerly worked for the BBC making some 30 films.

In February 1991—26 months before the murder of Stephen Lawrence brought racist murders in the London Borough of Greenwich to public attention—my teenage son Rolan was the first of four black people murdered by white killers. Rolan was attacked by a 15-strong gang of racist cowards. His younger brother Nathan escaped. The police and Crown Prosecution Service connived to remove the racist element from the crimes. Only Mark Thornburrow was convicted of the murder.

As a victim of institutional racism I quickly saw the injustice of the case of the Cardiff Five and came to appreciate and admire the work that Satish Sekar put in on that case especially. He cared about all of the victims of that injustice and others too. Twenty years later he continues to fight for justice. His role in that case was pivotal—having worked not only to free the innocent, but to bring the guilty to justice. Even after making history in that respect he continues to fight on to bring to book the system that allowed so gross an injustice to happen. I met the late Yusef Abdullahi and worked with him as well as Satish. It was tragic to learn what happened to Yusef and to think of the failure to restore him to the life he should have had.

In his case there is no doubt that he was a victim of crime as well and should have received every support available, yet he was left to rot by a system that had wronged him, his co-accused and Lynette's family terribly. There are forgotten or ignored victims of crime. My family has first-hand experience of that. I appreciated Satish's often unseen efforts to help all of the victims. Twenty years after we met in horrible circumstances we remain friends and working together. Sadly, the battle against injustice that brought us together remains to be won

Richard Adams is the father of Rolan Adams

To the memory of Yusef Abdullahi, Ronnie Actie, Peggy Pesticcio, Ursula Turner, Mahmood Mattan and Richard Lewis (Dic Penderyn).

Dic's case meets all the standards of vindication yet more than 180 years after his wrongful execution he remains convicted of a crime he did not commit. There is no excuse for the authorities not to quash this conviction and they should do so without further delay.[1]

The End of the Beginning

OVER A DECADE AGO MY book telling the story of one of Britain's most notorious miscarriages of justice, *Fitted In: The Cardiff Three and the Lynette White Inquiry*, was published.[1] It helped to make legal history several times over, and rapidly achieved its purpose of the re-opening of the police inquiries with a view to finding the real murderer.

Within five years of publication, Jeffrey Gafoor, the first murderer to be trapped by DNA-testing into pleading guilty, thereby resolving a notorious miscarriage of justice in the process, was brought to justice. That had never been achieved before, but some of the vital lessons are in danger of being lost in the overwhelming interest caused by more recent events in the case. That is understandable, but the story of how the case was solved, how this could assist in other cases, the injustice over the minimum terms that the innocent and guilty were given to serve in jail for the same offence — and much more besides — deserves to be brought to the attention of the public.

Even nowadays these things remain neglected. Gafoor turned out to be incredibly dangerous — a killer whose actions could not be predicted, as his behaviour defied precedent. The CJS has so far failed to take notice of this and devise strategies accordingly. The consequences of discovering killers like Gafoor, along with the concept and importance of vindication,[2] offer

---

1. (1997), London: Fitted In Project.
2. Vindication in this context means a proven miscarriage of justice where there is no doubt whatsoever about innocence, because either it can be proved that no crime occurred (for example an expert wrongly claiming a death was homicide, when natural causes or accident was more likely on the scientific evidence) or the real killer is brought to justice after a miscarriage of justice is revealed. I include here cases where the real killer is dead if there is compelling evidence of guilt that is accepted at official level, or clearly should be, as in the case of Richard Lewis (aka Dic Penderyn). Another example is David Lace, who committed suicide in 1984. Sean Hodgson was innocent. DNA-testing eventually proved this and, after exhumation, Lace was implicated in the rape and murder of Teresa di Simone, but he was dead and could never stand trial. Hampshire Police accept that Lace was the real killer. It would be perverse not to consider Hodgson vindicated in these circumstances.

lessons too important for the future of justice to ignore. There is much more besides — hence this book.

A Notorious Miscarriage of Justice

Five innocent men — Yusef Abdullahi, John and Ronnie Actie, Stephen Miller and Tony Paris — stood trial for the brutal murder of 20-year-old Lynette White, which occurred in the early hours of Valentine's Day 1988. In November 1990 the Actie cousins were acquitted and the others, who became known as the Cardiff Three, were sentenced to life imprisonment after the then longest murder trial in British history ended in Swansea's Guildhall. They received tariffs — the minimum duration that they must serve in prison before becoming eligible for release — that would prove controversial later, as the real murderer, Jeffrey Gafoor, received a more lenient one.

On December 10th 1992 Abdullahi, Miller and Paris had their convictions quashed on appeal with the ringing endorsement of the then Lord Chief Justice, Lord Taylor, but there was no apology. Many questions remained unanswered, including the most important — what their innocence meant. If they didn't kill Lynette, who did? When the Cardiff Three were freed no miscarriage of justice had ever been resolved in Britain by the conviction of the truly guilty in a murder case. Nevertheless, I was convinced that this case was solvable and that the memory of Lynette White deserved no less, so I set out to persuade the authorities to resolve it. That was the main point of writing my earlier book. The other was to ensure that the lessons of a grave miscarriage of justice were learned, but that would have to wait. This case simply refused to go away until and unless it was correctly resolved — and not even then, but the Lynette White Inquiry was not an isolated example of a miscarriage of justice in South Wales.

A Pattern of Concern

Several miscarriages of justice have served to affect confidence in South Wales Police and the CJS. Two previous ones had dire consequences: the execution of innocent men.[3] Fortunately the Cardiff Five case is from a different era, but they had a long wait for vindication, which would come from an unexpected source and in a manner nobody had anticipated, courtesy of South Wales Police themselves. This book details how that happened and the lessons it offers. Several other convictions had been overturned on appeal or resulted in acquittals in circumstances suggesting that arrests had been a miscarriage of justice, but the wait for acknowledgement of innocence, let alone vindication, had been a long one and up to then in vain.

Two of the Cardiff Five, John and Ronnie Actie were as innocent as the three who had been wrongly convicted, but the hopes for vindication of all five men seemed little more than a pipe dream at the start and would not have happened had it not been for the other cases I mention above contributing to the considerable pressure for a public inquiry, which grew in the year after the publication of my earlier book. Michael O'Brien had been the victim of one of Wales' most notorious miscarriages of justice, losing over a decade of his life; he emerged as the leading advocate for a public inquiry.

I started the calls for a public inquiry in May 1999 and others took up the cudgels regarding their own cases, but two cases were shamefully excluded. Mahmood Mattan was the last person executed in Cardiff Prison. He was innocent and the victim of an appalling miscarriage of justice that was on every level an affront to justice. Disgracefully it took 46 years to quash his conviction, but it wasn't the only miscarriage of justice that was ignored. One-hundred-and-twenty-one years earlier Richard Lewis (Dic Penderyn) was also executed for a crime he did not commit. His case was not even mentioned. Why not? As the former Governor of Maryland, Parris Glendening aptly said when pardoning John Snowden in May 2001 due to inconsistencies in the case, 82 years after his wrongful execution,

> The search for justice has no statute of limitations. When faced with the possible miscarriage of justice, even from the distant past, our values compel us to take a second look.[4]

---

3.   See further below and also in *Chapter 1* and *Appendix 1*.

4.   Snowden was hanged on February 28th, 1919 for the murder of Lottie Mae Brandon in her home almost 19 months earlier. It was a controversial case even then. Brandon was white, while Snowden was black and Snowden had been brutalised by police. Despite a petition for

Quite right.

I thought that excluding those cases was shameful and still do. Victims of miscarriages of justice had imposed a statute of limitations on the search for justice. The consequences of those miscarriages were the worst of all. There was no triumphant fist-waving in the air walk to freedom for them. There was no return to their families or relatives. There was no investigation of how British justice had judicially murdered innocent men. There was no redress for decades of pain that their families had suffered. The stigma they had borne with fortitude and dignity had been insulted by people who should have known better.

Excluding the cases of Mahmood Mattan and Richard Lewis from the calls for a public inquiry was a mistake, especially as Lewis was vindicated by the death-bed confession of Ianto Parker and the methods used to secure those convictions are strikingly similar to those complained about here. In addition to that, focusing exclusively on South Wales Police was a mistake: it let the rest of the cjs that had tolerated, or even encouraged the methods complained about, off the hook—but some would not budge, so a golden opportunity was lost. Despite disagreement on its focus, there can be no doubt that the campaign that O'Brien led achieved some notable results, including helping to give the Cardiff Five the thing he wanted most for himself—vindication.

The Unit

The reputation of South Wales Police took a hiding in an event-filled month, May 1999. The clamour for a public inquiry became deafening, but behind the scenes they had already been taking notice of developments and not just over these cases. In May 1999 assistant chief constable (ACC) Tony Rogers, who has since retired, announced the formation of a pioneering unit—the Major Crimes Review Unit (MCRU)—that came under the auspices of the Professional Standards Department. Its remit would be to review unsolved

---

the sentence to commuted signed by eleven of the 12 jurors, the then Governor, Emerson Harrington, refused. Snowden went to his death refusing to confess, telling his persecutors, "I could not leave this world with a lie on my lips".

and unresolved homicides. The Lynette White Inquiry was the first of the miscarriage of justice cases that it reviewed, although its first major success was an unsolved case — two actually.

Operation Magnum — the Llandarcy murders — would prove important to the Lynette White Inquiry as well, as the techniques required to solve these crimes did not exist when the murders occurred, but would be used to great effect in the Lynette White Inquiry as well. Unlike previous investigations they engaged critics and sought to convince them that the lessons had been learned. In this case their harshest independent critic had been me. They thought that if they could convince me that they had changed and were serious about investigating Lynette's murder impartially and effectively, then they could convince anyone that was willing to give them the opportunity to prove themselves and in the process they could restore public confidence in the force, which had taken a battering in the preceding year. After a review that lasted 15 months the Lynette White Inquiry was formally reopened in September 2000.

Painstaking research reduced the list of suspects to 100 in months, but there was still much work to do in both inquiries. The approach of researching familial DNA based on a hunch that relatives were likely to be criminally active and therefore on the National DNA Database proved invaluable in both investigations. They had far more material to work with in the Lynette White Inquiry as police had preserved several items, many of which bore the killer's DNA profile and Dave Barclay — then Head of Physical Evidence at the National Crime and Operations Faculty (NCOF) — reconstructed the exit route of the killer and his height too. An exceptional investigation both by police and forensic scientists followed a similar path to the Llandarcy and Skewen rapes and murders to resolution. The real murderer was not on the National DNA Database, but a close relative was. Gafoor was a careful killer, whose behavioural characteristics were impossible to predict. He had not been arrested for an offence since the National DNA Database was established either.[5]

---

5. Or his DNA would most likely have been stored. At that time, data could be retained of people who had been arrested even when they had not been convicted. Despite changes to the law, DNA-data of people who have not been convicted is still being kept.

Excellent work, especially by Professor Barclay to locate sources of DNA and innovative DNA work at Forensic Alliance gave forensic scientists the opportunity to shine. DNA from the murderer was discovered under paint almost 14 years after Lynette lost her life, but Gafoor had not committed any offence that would have allowed his DNA profile to be stored on the database and that meant that investigators could either wait and hope for the killer to reveal himself or they could investigate further.

Detective constable (DC) Paul Williams had a hunch of his own and chose the latter option—the same as John Whitaker's. Lynette's killer's DNA profile was not on the database. So what? It required familial DNA proving that the killer belonged to a particular family, but without the painstaking work of locating the areas that the killer would have deposited his DNA over a decade later, none of this could have assisted. One allele (band) in the killer's DNA profile was rare enough to eliminate 99% of people on the National DNA Database on its own. There were 70 relevant profiles, but one stood out. It belonged to a then 14-year-old criminally active boy. Police now knew that Lynette's killer was a male relative of this boy.

On July 4th 2003 South Wales Police made history again when Gafoor became the first British murderer to be jailed for his crime after a miscarriage of justice. While police forces share information, defence lawyers and campaigners still remain blissfully unaware of how useful the techniques used to resolve this murder could be in other cases. Miscarriages of justice could be among them, but there are other lessons to emerge from the discovery of Gafoor's guilt. He was a very frightening killer. He had no criminal record before Lynette's murder and the next four years revealed no crimes until an attack with half a brick on a work colleague. He never came to police attention again until his arrest for Lynette's murder almost eleven years later. This was not supposed to happen and had never been predicted in psychological traits. Killers built up to crimes like the sadistic murder of Lynette White and, once such blood lust had been awakened, it could not be shut off, but Gafoor denied every aspect of conventional wisdom concerning such crimes.

How could his actions be predicted and prevented? And how many other killers like Gafoor are still out there? The methods employed to bring him to justice are therefore of great importance, but there are other aspects of the Gafoor story that need to be highlighted.

Tariff Outrage

Only Jeffrey Gafoor knew for certain that he had murdered Lynette. He kept that knowledge to himself until attempting suicide in February 2003, as he knew then that his guilty secret had been discovered and he would have to face trial for his crime if he lived. His life was saved by police smashing in his door and taking him to hospital after he took a massive overdose of paracetamol, so Gafoor had to take responsibility for his crime and did so by pleading guilty to Lynette's murder, but he was treated more leniently than the men he acknowledged were innocent. Not only did he receive a smaller tariff than the Cardiff Three, but the system is set up to help him — a guilty man — achieve freedom while placing numerous obstacles in the path of the innocent. They could never have been released on parole at that time without admitting guilt and detailing how they carried out the crime that they did not commit. Either they would have been rewarded for a lie, which demanded further lies, or they would be punished further for maintaining the truth. They were expected to show remorse for a crime they did not commit — remorse that would have prevented this case from being investigated and Gafoor being brought to justice.

Gafoor was also given credit for a swift guilty plea over 15 years after the sadistic murder of Lynette White, even though he knew full well that innocent men had lost 16 years of their lives in jail for a crime that he admitted that he committed on his own and that they had emerged to a prison without bars where they were unjustly stigmatised for another decade. He hid the truth and was then credited further for assisting police in an inquiry that his silence helped to cause. He also benefited from an absurd categorisation of the crime. The murder involved over 50 stab wounds, some cutting to the bone; her throat had also been slit twice. Incredibly the trial judge described this murder as "verging on the sadistic". If this is not sadistic, what is? Mr Justice (Sir John) Royce's decision drastically reduced the tariff that he set on Gafoor, because sadism affects the starting point of tariffs. It could have been 30 years minimum if it had been described as sadistic, double the starting point that Royce chose. What kind of message does this send to killers? And that does not even take into account what Royce considered the most important aggravating circumstance, allowing innocent men to go to prison for a crime that Gafoor knew he had committed.

Gafoor did not wrongly accuse the Cardiff Five, but he chose to say nothing when he knew for certain that he alone was guilty. He truly has a lot to be remorseful about, but he could play a system that was designed to help the guilty while punishing the innocent. He can not only show it, but be rewarded for doing so. He can do all the courses necessary to show that he deserves release at the first opportunity, which could mean that he actually serves less time in prison for his crime than the innocent men he allowed to go to prison for it. What kind of justice is that? Nevertheless, the government has no plans to criminalise or even penalise such behaviour. Why would any murderer take responsibility for their crimes—even at the expense of the innocent—if they can expect more lenient treatment by staying silent? There is absolutely no incentive to take responsibility for murders, or even deterrence, in the tariff system. Despite years passing since Gafoor received his tariff (13 years, including time spent on remand), both the previous and current government refused to remedy this scandalous state of affairs that betrays the memory of Lynette White and disgraces the CJS and the politicians that tolerate it.

The Cardiff Five were the first to be vindicated in the DNA age in Britain and tariff reform should have been the start of improvements to the CJS that helps prevent miscarriages of justice and punishes the truly guilty justly, but this is far from everything that vindication can and should achieve. Vindication opened the door to real justice a process that does not end with Gafoor's conviction. It starts with it.

CHAPTER 1

PRESSURE — A FORCE TO BE RECKONED WITH

A Daunting Task

IT WAS THE MOST VICIOUS knife killing that the Welsh capital had ever seen and something had to be done to catch the murderer. Twenty-year-old Lynette White was killed on St Valentine's Day 1988 in the flat at 7 James Street in the Butetown district of Cardiff where she used to entertain punters; she had been stabbed more than 50 times.

Jeffrey Gafoor slit her throat twice and continued stabbing her as she was dying or dead. It was sadistic and far beyond what was needed to kill. Such a brutal killer had to be brought to justice and quickly, but it could not be achieved then as forensic science had to catch up and Gafoor was not a suspect at that time, because he had no criminal record and his use of prostitutes had passed unnoticed. There was no reason for the police to be aware of him in 1988. He committed that awful crime and then got on with his life, blotting out what had happened, staying silent while a gross miscarriage of justice that blighted several lives was allowed to occur.

John and Ronnie Actie spent two years on remand for a crime that they did not commit—they were acquitted in November 1990, but they and their families never recovered from the traumatic experience. Two years later Yusef Abdullahi, Stephen Miller and Tony Paris (the Cardiff Three) had their convictions quashed on appeal. They never recovered either. Ronnie Actie died in tragic circumstances in September 2007 the first of the wrongly accused men to do so. Lynette's father, Terry, was already dead. He did not support the process of re-opening the case, but it had to be done.

The evidence conclusively proved that the Cardiff Five were innocent. Gafoor admitted that he had murdered Lynette and that he had done it alone. However, there were serious consequences of the fact of their innocence. It meant that not only had justice miscarried, but also that the real killer was still free and such killers tend not to stop once the blood lust had been awakened. While the wrong men languished in jail, there was no investigation of who really killed Lynette and that meant that the public was still at risk.

I first got involved in this case in 1991, but freeing the Cardiff Three was not enough. They still had to live with the stigma of an unjust accusation; society remained at risk; Lynette and her family had been cheated of justice and the CJS, not just South Wales Police, had failed. Justice and the memory of Lynette White demanded and deserved better, so I continued my investigation, knowing that history had to be made and there had to be a change in mindset throughout the CJS. There were several battles to fight. The murder inquiry had to be re-opened twice and Jeffrey Gafoor had to be exposed for the brutal murderer that he was, but that required many things starting with pressure to investigate thoroughly. There had been several miscarriages of justice in South Wales; a change had to come.

The Precedent

A decade after the murder of Lynette White, the Cardiff Three have long since been freed and the quest for justice has moved on. Lynette's natural mother, Peggy Pesticcio, was still fighting for justice for her daughter, but this was not an isolated example of justice miscarrying in South Wales. It was just one of the first wrongful convictions in Wales to be overturned on appeal. There had also been acquittals in inappropriate prosecutions and allegations about the methods used. This stretched back decades—even before the foundation of the present force, but none of these miscarriages could have happened if the CJS had not somehow failed to rein matters in by enforcing the standards that the law demands—it wasn't just the police, the system seemed to be dysfunctional.

The movement for change started with demands for a public inquiry into some of the cases which had been investigated. The Cardiff Five would eventually be vindicated—have their innocence confirmed by the conviction of the real killer. They were the first people to achieve that status in the DNA-age in Britain. They were undoubtedly the first in Wales to be vindicated, weren't they? Well, that depends on the definition of vindication. Richard Lewis (Dic Penderyn) was judicially murdered by the British state 180 years ago. Forty-three years after Lewis was slowly hanged in Cardiff Market, Ianto Parker confessed on his death-bed to the Reverend Evan Evans that he had committed the crime that cost Penderyn his life. Death-bed confessions have been accepted as evidence previously, but at that time there was no means to quash Lewis' conviction (though he could have been given a posthumous pardon, but even that was not forthcoming). It remains a shameful blot on British justice. However, Lewis is not the only man to be wrongfully executed in the Welsh capital.

Mahmood Mattan[1] also paid the ultimate price and the methods used to convict him were scandalous and tragic as they were lethally effective and at that time had been passed down the ranks. In a more modern era, the Cardiff Three, Newsagents Three (below) and many others too could have shared his fate, despite being completely innocent.

The Transition to PACE

Mattan was hanged in the 1950s — a time when a police officer's word was law and mistakes were not resolved. Confessions had been extracted with violence and if that didn't work suspects could be verballed — 'confessions' in cars or even cells without legal protection. In the early 1970s the Maxwell Confait Inquiry highlighted these problems and also the need to protect vulnerable suspects.

The Police and Criminal Evidence Act 1984 (PACE) became law six years after the Royal Commission that would vindicate Colin Lattimore, Ronald Leighton and Ahmet Salih began. It took two further years to become law, but the transition was difficult, especially in South Wales. The longest-lasting miscarriage of justice in Welsh history began in this period. It was the misfortune of the Newsagents Three that their case occurred too soon. There were over a hundred abuses of PACE, but it took a decade for the importance of these breaches, which included off-the-record interviews and handcuffing a vulnerable suspect to hot radiators, to be realised and acted on. The

---

1. For further information on Mattan and (Lewis) Penderyn, see *Appendix 1*, "Judicial Murder" and for some of the other cases mentioned, see *Appendix 2*, "Some Further Injustices".

on-the-record interviews were not tape-recorded and that had major consequences too. Canton Police Station did not have the facilities to record interviews at the time. Why not? PACE had been operational for almost two years at the time. Now, even interviews with witnesses are tape-recorded, but a fleet of coach and horses had been driven through the legislation and its spirit in the Phillip Saunders Inquiry.

Detective superintendent Alan Partridge of Thames Valley Police was commissioned by the Criminal Cases Review Commission (CCRC) to review South Wales Police's investigation of the murder of Phillip Saunders. He found several breaches of the law. Freedom wasn't long in coming for the Newsagents Three. However, some of the breaches should have been exposed far earlier. Solicitors had witnessed the handcuffing of clients to hot radiators. There can be no excuse for such conduct or the failure to expose it at trial. In December 1998 Darren Hall, Michael O'Brien and Ellis Sherwood were granted bail pending their appeal against their convictions for the October 1987 murder of newspaper vendor Phillip Saunders.[2] The appeal centred on the unreliability of the confession of Darren Hall — an extremely vulnerable person — and claims of bad faith on the part of South Wales Police, especially Stuart Lewis, who retired with the rank of detective chief inspector (DCI), in several cases, especially the Cardiff Explosives Conspiracy trials. There were other cases in the 1980s that resulted in acquittals which raised serious questions of integrity, such as those of Anthony Yellen and Sharon Kelleher. However, there was a bigger problem than Lewis. Don Carsley was also involved in both cases and went on to become the head of South Wales Police's Criminal Investigation Department (CID), but unlike Lewis he could have faced prosecution over another miscarriage of justice the Darvell brothers (Paul and Wayne). This was another transition case, where PACE had allegedly been complied with, despite it not being required by law. Sadly, it took seven years to prove that judge and jury had been shamefully deceived. Lord Taylor delivered a swingeing judgement at their 1992 appeal, although three police officers were subsequently acquitted of conspiracy to pervert the course of justice.

---

2. For further details of the Newsagents Three, see *The Death of Justice: Guilty Until Proven Innocent* (2008), Michael O'Brien and Greg Lewis, Talybont: Y Lolfa.

There were other miscarriages of justice in South Wales that contributed to the clamour for a public inquiry. The methods used in these cases were similar as well. Plainly there was a problem, but was it restricted to the transitional period and the police alone? Questions needed to be asked of other agencies too. Did these cases fit the criteria for prosecution of the Code for Crown Prosecutors? If not, why had these cases been approved for prosecution at all? The Crown Prosecution Service (CPS) had been established in 1986 to ensure that decisions on whether to prosecute or not would be independent of the police. Was the CPS doing its job to the standard the public had a right to expect and demand? Seven years later a case began that provided some answers.

The Post-PACE Act Cases

The PACE Act transition period was well and truly over when Harry and Megan Tooze were shot dead at their farm-house in South Wales in July 1993. Their daughter Cheryl's boyfriend Jonathan Jones — they have since married — was subsequently charged with their murders. An entirely circumstantial case resulted in Jones being wrongfully convicted. Like the other cases, there was no credible scientific evidence against him, but Jones' case was unusual in that it didn't completely fit the pattern of the others. Jones was not vulnerable and nor were the witnesses. Those accusing him freely chose to give the evidence that they did, although the investigation of his alibi was a different matter and the significance of the scientific evidence was overestimated at best.

The evidence against Jones was weak, so his conviction was surprising, so much so that the trial judge, the late Mr Justice (Sir Richard) Rougier, wrote to Jones' defence counsel, John Charles Rees QC, including concerns that the prosecution, led by Christopher Pitchford QC, had not proved guilt, although Rougier's stewardship of the trial was criticised strongly by Rees at appeal as well. To Rougier's annoyance his comments were made public and Jones was freed on appeal in May 1996. The case against him had been weak and unusual compared to the pattern of the other miscarriages of justice. Nevertheless, Jones was not the only person prosecuted on flimsy evidence. The Court of Appeal refused to rule Jones' prosecution inappropriate and the next one slipped by unnoticed at the time, but the one after bucked the trend. Diane Jones and her young children Shauna and Sarah-Jane Hibberd died in a fire at their home on the Gurnos Estate in Merthyr Tydfil in October 1995.

The following year three local women, Donna Clarke, Annette Hewins and Denise Sullivan were charged over their deaths. Everyone (police, prosecution and defence lawyers) accepted that Hewins was at home in bed when the fire happened. The case against her was that she took Clarke to a garage earlier that night and bought petrol that she allegedly gave to Clarke. It wasn't even proved that the petrol she bought from that garage was used in the fire. No trace of the leaded component of petrol, tetraethyl lead, was recovered from any of the fire debris or samples tested. That is important because CCTV footage shows Hewins buying leaded petrol that night. Unusually, the police were not entirely convinced of her guilt, but her prosecution raised several new issues, such as the cracking of Clarke's alibi at the expense of the spirit of PACE and the unlawful use of hearsay evidence to secure Hewins' conviction. She received neither apology, exoneration nor compensation in a case that the Court of Appeal judges said should never have come to trial in the first place, but the same year that Hewins was wrongfully convicted, Phillip Skipper stood trial for the March 1996 murder of his estranged wife Karen. This was also a flimsy case that had something in common with that against Hewins. Despite tunnel-vision police did not think they had gathered enough evidence to secure a conviction. They were proved right in 1997.

Cranking up the Pressure

Along with the proven miscarriage of justice cases (which include some inappropriate charges that led to acquittals such as those of two of the Cardiff Five) concerns had been raised about the quality of the investigations in several other cases such as that of the late Patrick McCann. His case was referred back for appeal, but despite strong evidence and legal argument, his appeal was rejected. There had been investigations of the methods used in these cases, but many of them lacked credibility because they exonerated the original investigations without unearthing material that led to successful appeals. In some cases, they exonerated colleagues whose methods had been criticised in successful appeals. The Lynette White Inquiry was an example of this. Nobody believed in it as the so-called investigations had been conducted by colleagues of the officers who had originally investigated these cases. However, the tide was turning against such investigations. The media, lawyers and campaigners had come to believe that there was a serious institutional problem that had to be dealt with.

I was among the first to call for a fully independent public inquiry into these cases, but the problem was, in my view, not just policing. Before the Prosecution of Offenders Act 1985 established the CPS, police not only arrested suspects, but decided whether they would be prosecuted as well. In 1986 the CPS took over that responsibility; it had to decide whether there was enough reliable evidence to give a realistic chance of persuading a jury to convict and whether prosecuting was in the public interest. There were criteria that Crown prosecutors had to consider before deciding whether to prosecute or not, but the CPS was proving in practice that it was compliant at best and failing to function as intended. It approved four prosecutions that were subsequently overturned on appeal and in each of them there were strong reasons to suggest that these prosecutions and at least one other should never have been brought. Was the CPS genuinely independent of the police, or was it justifying arrests with inappropriate prosecutions? The case against Hewins was weak and her conviction was secured by inadmissible evidence. During her appeal it emerged that she should not have been charged at all; the CPS and the member of Queen's Counsel it instructed should have known that and stopped the prosecution before it began.

There were issues over the use or even manipulation of forensic science in many of these cases as well. Although there is no guarantee that murderers will leave scientific evidence behind that can tie them to their crimes, there was nothing that tied any of these defendants to the scene of the crime or the victims in circumstances where there ought to have been if the defendants were guilty as charged. Forensic science not only suggested that it was unlikely that they were involved in these crimes, but possibly offered new investigators the chance to make history by resolving these cases with the conviction of the truly guilty. It was a daunting task. No miscarriage of justice had ever been resolved in Britain by the conviction of the real killer, but for any of these cases to be resolved correctly there had to be material to test. The most likely cases that could be solved in South Wales were those of Sandra Phillips and Lynette White. Others were possible too, but before any of them could be solved two things had to happen. Forensic science had to catch up with the needs of these cases — there was limited and poor quality material to work with — and there had to be a sea-change in the attitude of the police. The former happened rapidly, but few believed that a sea-change in police attitudes was possible — hence the calls for a public inquiry.

CHAPTER 2

ADVANCES IN FORENSIC SCIENCE

A Substantial Clue — Blood Grouping

Lynette white's murder which happened in Flat 1 at 7 St James Street, Butetown, Cardiff was especially brutal. It was a frenzied knife attack that involved at least 50 stab wounds. Her throat had been slit with such force that the blade had hit the spine. There were two deep cuts to the throat—one horizontal and the other diagonal. She didn't stand a chance. Those wounds alone made death inevitable unless she received prompt treatment, but her life was in the hands of a callous killer. Even after these wounds had been inflicted Jeffrey Gafoor continued to stab the defenceless and by then probably lifeless Lynette dozens of times. It was a vicious crime that went far beyond what was necessary to kill. He attacked her breasts and slashed her wrists when she was dead or close to death. Why? Gafoor's account of his crime beggared belief. He explained through his Queen's Counsel, John Charles Rees that he had accompanied Lynette to the flat for sex, but changed his mind after paying her £30. He claimed that he demanded the return of his money, which she refused and he lost his temper.

The extent of damage to Lynette's body went far beyond such a cause. A dispute over £30 does not begin to explain such a brutal attack and nor has Gafoor. Behavioural analysis that was pioneered by the Federal Bureau of Investigation (FBI) in Quantico, Virginia made great strides in understanding the motivation and behaviour of criminals, but even today nobody can explain this crime, which helped to make it so hard to detect in 1988. Nevertheless, there was a substantial clue that should at least have prevented a miscarriage of justice from happening. The knife hit bone with such force that the murderer's hand slid down the handle, by now slippery with Lynette's blood, onto the blade, cutting him. Numerous blood-stained items were recovered from the scene of the crime during the original investigation. Some of them were subjected to conventional blood grouping tests — and almost all of the blood was found to have been shed by Lynette. That was hardly surprising given the ferocity of the attack that took her life. However, there were some blood-stains that could not have been shed by her, as they did not match her combination of blood groups; they had clearly been deposited there during the murder, so these were significant clues.

Traces of this "foreign" blood-staining were discovered on the bottom of Lynette's jeans and on one of her socks.[1] The investigation initially proceeded on the basis that Lynette had been murdered by one man acting alone, as the scientific scene analysis indicated. A then novel test also established that the male Y-chromosome was present on one area of the blood-stain on her jeans, confirming the original interpretation. The blood grouping evidence was a major clue. The combination of the six groups analysed was only found in 1:3,800 of the population. That meant that approximately 16,000 people in Britain possessed that combination of groups — approximately half of whom could be eliminated because they were women. There was no way of telling exactly how many of 8,000 men in Britain who possessed that rare combination of blood groups lived in Cardiff, or within commuting distance of the Welsh capital. Nevertheless, it was a significant clue — one that allowed police to eliminate many people. That was a courtesy that ought to have been extended to the Cardiff Five as well. They were the only people who were not eliminated on blood grouping evidence that ought to have been as their combination of blood groups were vastly different from that of the killer. Blood grouping evidence ought to have prevented a miscarriage of justice from happening to them.

Plenty of physical evidence had been collected by scenes of crime officers (SOCOs) and forensic scientists. This included blood-staining on items, walls and the carpet. There were also hairs, fibres, trainer-prints and fingerprints. None of this evidence tied any of the Cardiff Five to the flat or victim and none of it showed that more than one person — an unknown male — was present. While the absence of scientific evidence proves nothing on its own, this was different. There were traces of the killer in that flat and it did not match any of the men who stood trial. It proved them innocent. Forensic

---

1. In this context, "foreign blood" means blood that was not shed by Lynette White.

science had eliminated them as viable suspects, but a miscarriage of justice still occurred as an erroneous case hypothesis was allowed to over-ride the scientific evidence.

DNA

The blood grouping evidence should have established that the Cardiff Five were innocent, but the investigation changed tack from one killer to five, even though, scientifically, this did not make sense. There were no traces of any of the Cardiff Five in the flat or on the victim. In fact, it was acknowledged even in court that the scientific evidence proved that if the Cardiff Five had been involved then there had to have been a sixth man as well that none of the witnesses had mentioned, let alone named. One man acting on his own was far more likely, and was the original assessment of the forensic scientist and supported by all the evidence. This was subsequently proved true 15 years later, but the Lynette White Inquiry took a wrong track first. The Cardiff Five were arrested in December 1988. It was their misfortune that police discovered through another case that Angela Psaila—she would become a crucial witness—possessed the same combination of blood groups as the killer.

The senior scientific officer at the Chepstow Laboratory, who was in charge of the scientific work, Dr. John Whiteside, described this as, "One hell of a coincidence". But why was it ever anything more than coincidence? Approximately 16,000 people possessed that combination of blood groups and all bar one of them had nothing to do with the murder. Even more importantly, police knew that the person who shed that blood in the flat was male. Dr. Peter Gill's Y-chromosome test detected the male chromosome and Psaila did not possess it. Nevertheless, she was persuaded into believing that her blood had indeed been discovered in the flat. She was genuinely surprised when she was told almost 15 years later that her blood had not been found there after all.

In 1988, DNA-testing was comparatively young as an investigative tool in the fight against crime. Colin Pitchfork was the first criminal to be convicted as a result of this method. It has to be corroborated by other evidence.

Pitchfork raped and murdered schoolgirls Linda Mann and Dawn Ashworth. An innocent man Richard Buckland confessed to one of the crimes, but vehemently denied the other. Alec Jeffreys (later Professor Sir Alec Jeffreys) believed that he could establish the truth behind Buckland's seemingly contradictory claims, even though the technique had only been used to resolve paternity issues until then. Jeffreys was confident that DNA could distinguish between two individuals unless they were identical twins. To the surprise of investigators Jeffreys proved their belief that the crimes were committed by the same person to be true, but also that Buckland was not that man. DNA-testing had never been used in a criminal case, but before it helped to tie Pitchfork to his crimes, it proved Buckland's innocence. Pitchfork was eventually trapped when a friend, Ian Kelly, boasted that he had taken the DNA-test for him and been paid for it. Pitchfork was arrested and the DNA-test verified that his DNA was consistent with the person who had raped and murdered the schoolgirls. He was jailed for life in January 1988.[2]

The same testing system was used in the Lynette White Inquiry, but before the samples were sent off for DNA analysis, fingerprinting experts got their chance. All of the eliminations on DNA were achieved from just two bloodstains on the wall near the area of the room where Lynette was murdered. Both stains had been treated with a fingerprinting chemical called ninhydrin. It subsequently emerged that the fingerprinting chemicals affected DNA. Degradation also affected DNA. Nevertheless, it was clear that the DNA profiles obtained from these stains did not match any of the Cardiff Five, but unlike other suspects that were eliminated on blood grouping tests, while the single male killer acting alone case-scenario was investigated by the police, the Cardiff Five were not eliminated on that basis or on the basis of DNA-testing either. It was already too late, as they were in prison on remand when the DNA-tests were conducted on them and excluded them. A scenario that defied logic was advanced to explain evidence that was now more than just an inconvenience, that involved Psaila's blood. However, her DNA had not been recovered from the relevant samples either.

---

2. Pitchfork was originally given a 30 year tariff, but challenged it and won a reduction of two years, based on his charity work. To the anger of his victims' families, he will be eligible to apply for parole in 2016.

The DNA profiles obtained from these stains were incomplete and a forensic scientist, Mark Webster, would later verify that the victim could not be eliminated solely on DNA as a potential source of some of those stains, on which no blood grouping tests had been conducted. This would later prove the need for a more integrated approach — blood distribution patterns were important too, but ignored. In terms of the information then available nobody could be eliminated on the basis of these DNA-tests on some, but not all of, the stains, but that information was applied selectively. On that basis it should have affected every single elimination achieved by DNA at that time, not just those of the Cardiff Five. This would eventually prove to be significant, but the scientific evidence was not allowed to speak truly at the trial, although it would later emerge that the blood had been shed by just one person and that he was the killer, meaning that the eliminations of everyone else by DNA, including the Cardiff Five, was reliable. Nevertheless, the way that the DNA results were manipulated to try to implicate the Cardiff Five against the evidence was shocking even at that time. Both it and especially the blood grouping tests should have eliminated the Cardiff Five without question.

Advances in DNA-testing Systems

In 1988, DNA was in its infancy and the system used at the time was neither as sensitive nor discriminating as current methods. Consequently, valuable DNA was used up without yielding useful results. The decision to prioritise fingerprinting at that time was justifiable, but ultimately DNA would prove the more useful. Nevertheless, the quality and quantity of DNA available was becoming an issue. The more tests that were conducted the less would be available as systems improved over time. However, defendants, especially those in prison, tend to want each and every test conducted on all items whether that suits the needs of the samples, case, or even their own interests.

As the 1980s gave way to the 1990s forensic science and its techniques continued to develop. Techniques were perfected to amplify small quantities of DNA into larger amounts, which enabled small stains to be tested. Some DNA-testing systems were not particularly discriminating and consequently were not likely to identify useful lines of enquiry, despite offering greater discrimination than the blood grouping tests. It could potentially eliminate more people and had it produced a definitive match, then it could have provided useful lines of enquiry, but one that was tried before the Cardiff Three were freed on appeal failed to yield any useful results. It was not particularly discriminating, so even if it had succeeded in yielding a full DNA profile the results may not have assisted greatly. However, it was followed by a significant breakthrough. Short-tandem-repeats (STR) typing combined a sensitive method of amplifying DNA, called Second Generation Multiplex (SGM), with a very discriminating type of DNA-test. It yielded a real possibility that useful DNA profiles could be obtained from even the poor quality DNA samples that existed in this case and others too. It offered a random match statistic — the possibility that the DNA being tested would randomly match another person — of 1:50 million. DNA-testing was catching up with the needs of the Lynette White Inquiry and would soon get an opportunity to resolve it.

Reopened

In April 1995 the Home Office was asked to take control of the Lynette White Inquiry. They refused, insisting that the only appropriate course was to refer it to the chief constable of South Wales Police. It proved to be an inappropriate option, but in October 1995 it was actively reopened by that force after the author's opinion that useful results could now be obtained was supported by Mark Webster. Peggy Pesticcio adopted these findings. Although they accepted that the Cardiff Five were innocent they refused to utilise the most sensitive method of amplifying DNA available at the time even though there was a limited supply of poor quality DNA. They also insisted that the decision on whether to use up the entire DNA in testing was for them to make. They completed an entire round of amplification with the less sensitive method, but no useful DNA profiles were obtained. It was a waste of time and resources involving precious DNA, that could have been avoided. It could have had dire consequences.

The poor quality of the DNA on the key samples in this case, the smear on Lynette's jeans and the cast-off blood spots that had not been shed by Lynette, was no secret, so it was not hard to predict that no useful results would be obtained. I had suggested that the needs of the samples in this inquiry were such that it was a case where the more sensitive method of amplification used by Professor Bernd Brinkmann of the University of Münster in Northern Germany could and possibly should have been used from the start, because valuable DNA had to be used to amplify it. DNA from crime scene samples was at a premium then and both it, time and resources were wasted needlessly. As techniques advanced the significance of this would diminish, but that could not have been known then. During 1997 it became clear that despite the advances in both amplification and DNA-testing, the available systems still were not sophisticated enough to unlock the secrets that the samples contained. Consequently, Pesticcio and I demanded that the testing stop in 1997, pending the development of amplification techniques and DNA-testing systems that could help to tie the real murderer of Lynette White to his crime. To their credit the police listened and suspended testing until that system had been developed. It wasn't a long wait.

The Prediction

DNA-testing had developed in leaps and bounds since the rudimentary system used in the original inquiry throughout the 1980s. In the mid-1990s the methods of amplifying DNA were not quite sensitive enough for the needs of the Lynette White Inquiry, but I was convinced that DNA held the key to correctly solving this brutal crime. I predicted that the day would come when a DNA-testing system would be developed that would be able to obtain useful evidence from samples that seemed useless at the time, even if they contained highly degraded and poor quality DNA, such as those in this inquiry.

However, it was imperative that there was DNA to amplify that could be tested when such a system was developed. It made no sense to test these samples to death. After all, it wasn't known then that there were other items that had been taken and stored that had the killer's DNA on them, nor was it known that 7 James Street still contained the killer's DNA preserved under paint. There was a very small supply of the killer's DNA that could still be tested when a suitable system was developed, but only if that DNA was preserved until then. Testing was suspended early in 1998 until such a system could be used. The delay was less than a year.

The Prediction Comes True

Applied Biosystems developed a DNA-testing system called SGM+ (Second Generation Multiplex Plus). It was used for the first time in 1998. The DNA-testing system that was then conducted remained STR typing,[3] but unlike its predecessor scientists had discovered how to amplify from a single cell—the smallest bearer of DNA. This meant that it was possible to multiply very small amounts of DNA without risking creating artefacts that would give false results. Amplification uses original DNA, but it was now possible to obtain DNA to test from smaller amounts and by testing at ten genes, rather than the six used previously, this system was more discriminating too. The possibility of a random match was now 1:1,000 million.

It might therefore be possible to obtain useful DNA evidence even from the seemingly useless samples that existed in the Lynette White Inquiry, just over a decade after her horrific murder, but advances in forensic science alone were not enough to make legal history. After a sub-standard scientific investigation that contributed to a miscarriage of justice, it would have to reclaim the reputation of forensic science by achieving something that no British police force or forensic scientists had succeeded in doing—resolving a miscarriage of justice by proving the guilt of the real murderer, but that required many things. They had time and the correct DNA-testing system, but before it could be tried the whole of the scientific evidence had to be reviewed in order to ensure that useful lines of investigation had not been missed.

The National Crime and Operations Faculty (NCOF) was established in 1996 as a resource for the police to ensure that useful lines of investigation were not missed by investigators, following concerns about the Yorkshire Ripper and Black Panther murder inquiries. It consisted of operational detectives, scientists and crime analysts working together to support live investigations and review previous cases. It was exactly what was needed in

---

3. Short Tandem Repeats.

52

any reinvestigation of Lynette White's murder and would have a vital role to play in the resolution of this case. DNA was also a very important investigative tool in the case, but for it to achieve its full potential it must be part of an integrated approach to the use of forensic science in tandem with other techniques. That is one of the most important lessons of this case along with the role of the NCOF, which played a crucial part in the resolution of this crime, but before they could prove their worth a potentially more difficult hurdle had to be overcome.

Did South Wales Police have the will to investigate it thoroughly enough to achieve the result of resolving a miscarriage of justice by the conviction of the truly guilty person, knowing that it might open up a can of worms the like of which none of the 43 police forces in England or Wales had ever experienced?

APPENDIX TO CHAPTER 2

Professor Dave Barclay

My involvement with the proven miscarriage of justice now known as the Cardiff Three (or Cardiff Five) arose out of my role as Head of Physical Evidence at the National Crime Faculty. The NCF assisted South Wales Police in several major reviews of the case and its consequences, starting with the new investigation in 1999 which led directly to the identification of Jeffrey Gafoor as the real offender.

Crime analysts, behavioural psychologists and physical evidence reviews all assisted the investigation, and some members of the NCF including myself were also involved with the Lay Advisory Group (see *Chapter 4*). My own role continued after the conviction of Gafoor when I undertook a detailed examination of the forensic science processes and interpretations made back in 1988 and 1989.

The forensic science in the Lynette White murder case seems complex at first sight. It comprises a combination of pathology, scene analysis, bloodgrouping, finger-marks, several varieties of DNA and novel tests for the Y-chromosome (male). It certainly seems complex in the way Satish Sekar has had to describe it. It is not.

From the very start the lead scientist, Dr. John Whiteside, identified some of the blood at the scene as "cast off" — originating from the offender because his hand had slipped down the blood-slippery knife onto the blade during his frenzied and prolonged attack on Lynette. That blood possessed a rare combination of blood groups and was a major clue for the investigators. Further, because of the positions it was found in, that blood could be used to eliminate suspects — it had to have been left by the offender. And because Lynette had bled profusely onto the floor and the flat was dark, it was inconceivable that multiple offenders were involved. Not only had no forensic trace of them been found, but also not one of the six or seven people, who must on the police's version have been milling about in the darkened flat, had trodden in her blood and left bloody footmarks.

But as far as the scientist was concerned, multiple offenders were irrelevant — his scene analysis was simple and certain and entirely correct — this was a stabbing attack by an offender who had cut himself. *Him*self because this was a typically male attack.

And for all the complicated further DNA, Y-chromosome and other analyses done prior to the first and second trials, no physical evidence at all emerged to contradict the single male theory held by Dr. Whiteside for so many months from February up to December 1988. And it never did emerge. The new DNA evidence that identified Jeffrey Gafoor as the offender and the locations that DNA was obtained from—cast off blood, grip marks on her jeans, fingermarks along the line of exit—were all in exact agreement with the original single male offender hypothesis.

So what went wrong? How could this very clear scientific picture have become so distorted that the prosecution was able to persuade a jury that the scientific findings supported an entirely mythical and scientifically ludicrous version of events?

The key event in this catalogue of errors happened when Angela Psaila was horrendously assaulted in late 1988. She was a known associate of Lynette White and possessed the same rare combination of blood groups. The scientist concerned was excited by this finding and from that moment on decided that the blood at the scene came from her.

Every subsequent test, whether Y-chromosome (the blood gave a male reaction) or DNA failed to support this new hypothesis or directly contradicted it, as did his own original crime scene analysis. But no matter, because as Lawrence Sterne wrote:

> It is the nature of an hypothesis, when once a man has conceived it, that it assimilates everything to itself as proper nourishment; and, from the first moment of your begetting it, it generally grows the stronger by everything you see, hear, read, or understand.

Once Dr. Whiteside had informed the police of his new hypothesis, of the link as he saw it between Psaila and the scene, the police took the actions which led directly to the Cardiff Five miscarriage of justice. And for his part Dr. Whiteside was apparently able to persuade himself that there were reasons to ignore the subsequent contradictory results. Those results were also expressed to the court in his statements and verbally to the jury in a way which was, at the least, less than clear.

The science became complex simply and only in order to explain away an obvious but inconvenient fact—that a single male stabbed Lynette White over 50 times; in so doing he cut his own hand and left his own blood in the flat exactly where you would expect. That person was Jeffrey Gafoor.

Professor Dave Barclay was formerly Head of Physical Evidence at the National Crime Faculty.

CHAPTER 3

THE UNIT: UNSOLVED AND UNRESOLVED HOMICIDES

Cold Cases

THE INVESTIGATION OF COLD CASES, often high profile ones, has been popularised by television dramas such as "Cold Case", "New Tricks" and "Waking the Dead". While these programmes raise awareness of the issues, real cold case work is vastly different. The odds are against solving these crimes as trails have not only gone cold, they are often frozen over. Nevertheless, modern investigators have many things in their favour—advances in forensic science, the use of psychology and crime analysis—but there are many barriers. Although re-investigations start from scratch, investigative opportunities could have been missed previously, so they can only be carried out fully if that lead was recorded in the original inquiry. The passage of time is a great hindrance too as memories fade; people move on with their lives and possibly away from the area and some may be dead.

Cold case investigations also depend on adequate storage of original material. Exhibits may have been previously examined and contaminated or poorly stored, so it may be more useful to try and retrieve completely new items from the scene even after ten or more years. Some police forces routinely destroy paperwork, although this should not be allowed to happen in unsolved or unresolved cases. Important papers can also be lost while archiving, or simply be mislaid. In the modern age case papers can be archived on computers, but there are dangers with this approach as well. Computer disks cannot be tested for fingerprints or DNA or by handwriting analysis of the original documents and they cannot be ESDA[1] tested either. Consequently, the originals should be kept indefinitely because forensic science could develop

---

1. Electrostatic depression analysis reveals indentations on paper, indicating previous versions of a document. In the late 1980s and 1990s it was used to show that notes claimed by police officers to have been recorded contemporaneously had not been so.

further techniques that reveal vital evidence in the future, but paperwork is only part of the problem.

DNA-testing has become an essential tool in the fight against crime. Crimes that could not be detected previously have been solved even if they occurred decades ago, but it depends on having original material to amplify and test and that depends on adequate storage of samples. Several agencies are involved, so paper trails are vital. In some cases police have responded to defence requests for material to test by informing them that it has been destroyed, genuinely believing that to be true, but that may not be accurate. Some material, even extracts from previous tests, may still be available for testing at the forensic science laboratories without police or lawyers realising it, but defence lawyers and investigators should be aware of this now and ensure that the paper trail has been exhausted before abandoning hope of further testing. While police obviously have advantages in terms of access to material there is no reason why those proclaiming innocence and their legal representatives cannot conduct their own research.

For example, Sean Hodgson was told more than a decade ago that there was no original material to DNA-test. His solicitor Julian Young pursued the matter and eventually material was found and tested that proved his innocence. It also offered new investigators the chance to solve the rape and murder of Teresa di Simone nearly 30 years after it happened. The DNA evidence obtained from that material not only proved Hodgson innocent—his convictions were quashed in March 2009—but six months later the real killer was identified and tied to his crime. David Lace committed suicide in 1984. His body was exhumed and DNA linked him to the crimes. Hampshire Police closed the file. If Young had not been so diligent, Hodgson—an innocent man—could still be in prison now.

Why Bother?

All forces in England and Wales have cold case units now, even though some people question the value of them. Why should resources and time be used investigating cases from many years ago? After all there are several major crimes that need investigating now and these historic cases are fraught with difficulties, but should there be a statute of limitations on justice? The victims of crime are entitled to justice however long it takes and even more so if there has been a miscarriage of justice in the case. Crimes, especially the most serious ones, leave a trail of devastated lives that affect real people, struggling to make sense of what happened and why. Justice is important for them, but also for society and of course, if the perpetrator has not been identified and convicted, he or she is free to offend again and again. Miscarriages of justice are worse because that results in extra victims. It is also a question that became personal to me. I never met Lynette White and before the convictions I had no idea who the Cardiff Five were and probably never would have met them or their families if they had not become victims of a notorious miscarriage of justice.

What happened to them did not affect me personally in any way whatsoever, but their stories took over almost two decades of my life and even now I can't fully explain why. It was an obvious miscarriage of justice that offended my sense of fairness and I knew that it was a case that was capable of affecting real change throughout the cjs. It didn't take long for me to know that the Cardiff Five were innocent and after reviewing the evidence I was also certain that they would have a strong basis for an appeal, but for me their release was only half the battle. The Cardiff Five were entitled to their lives back without the inevitable whispering campaign that accompanies almost all successful appeals or acquittals. The convictions were not simply unsafe or unsatisfactory — they were an affront to every concept of justice. They deserved to have their names totally cleared with an apology for their ordeal, and that required vindication. They eventually got it, but many things had to happen first.

The Quest for Vindication

When the Cardiff Three were freed on appeal many people congratulated me and told me to move on to the next case. I ignored them — the job was only half done at best. Freeing the Cardiff Three simply wasn't enough; there was a brutal killer out there who had enjoyed ill-deserved liberty for too long. He had to be brought to justice. That became my next quest. I realised that it was a case that could be solved correctly and I wasn't going to shut up until it was investigated properly. To the best of my knowledge I'm one of a small group of journalists who have helped expose miscarriages of justice and then helped the victim's family to pursue justice and get it. My first book on the case, *Fitted In: The Cardiff Three and the Lynette White Inquiry*, was published seven and-a-half years after I first became involved and within a year it had achieved its primary purpose—getting the case reopened and investigated thoroughly. The entire CJS seemed to be dysfunctional, but lessons would not and could not be learned until the Cardiff Five had been proved innocent beyond doubt and Lynette's family had the deserved comfort of knowing that the real killer was behind bars. But while I was busy chasing justice for all concerned in that case, police were investigating older cases and achieving important results that prove there is no time limit on justice, and nor should there be.

Making History

Former lorry driver Joseph Kappen died aged 49 in 1990. He took his guilty secret to the grave, but it was destined not to stay hidden. Kappen was a serial killer. Seventeen years before his death Kappen struck terror into the inhabitants of the village of Llandarcy in South Wales. In September 1973 he raped and murdered 16-year-olds Geraldine Hughes and Pauline Floyd, who worked in a local sewing factory. The crimes remained unsolved for three decades and could not have been cleared up until forensic science caught up with the demands of this case. Both young women had been strangled, bludgeoned and raped as well. Their bodies were found in a copse near Floyd's home. These were horrible crimes and South Wales Police quickly made them a priority with several detectives assigned to the case, but they had made a terrible mistake. Three months earlier a similar crime occurred. Like Hughes and Floyd, Sandra Newton was also 16 and returning home from a Saturday night out at a disco when she too was raped and murdered. It happened nearby, but despite the obvious similarities police suspected Newton's boyfriend—wrongly—so the crimes were not officially linked at this time. Numerous statements were taken, suspects investigated and the major lead—a white Austin 1100—was researched, but another crucial error regarding the car was not spotted in an age before computerised records made cross-referencing information an easy task that did not devour time and effort. The trail went cold and in 1974 the inquiry was wound down until it was reopened in January 2000. Meanwhile, the files were archived and the clothing stored at the Home Office's forensic science laboratory in Chepstow.

South Wales Police were determined to deliver justice to the victims and asked the National Crime and Operations Faculty (NCOF) to co-ordinate a complete fresh-start review. They faced a daunting task as no unsolved case had been resolved in Britain after such a long time. The original pathologist and crime-scene examiners sat down with scientists from Chepstow and the NCOF over several days and completely reinterpreted the scenes of all three murders and constructed a protocol to rework the physical exhibits from scratch. The three cases: Floyd, Hughes and Newton were thought to be linked, but there was no physical proof of this yet. Some DNA results had been obtained earlier as part of routine reworking of old samples, but it was complicated as it proved difficult to separate the genetic material of the killer from that of Geraldine Hughes and it was not even known whether several offenders had taken part. The reinterpretation of the crime-scenes by the review allowed a full profile to be obtained from Pauline Floyd's clothing once it had been tracked down. The National DNA Database was checked, but there was no direct hit to that profile.

DCI Paul Bethell—he has retired now, but works as a civilian investigator with South Wales Police on cold cases—was assigned to the case, but his budget only stretched to 500 DNA-tests. That meant he had to concentrate on the most likely 500 suspects. He noticed that there had been a series of unsolved rapes in Neath shortly after the murders of Hughes and Floyd that also involved tying up the victims. An offender profile was compiled that helped the new team narrow down their list of suspects. After several months they had decided on their 500 to be DNA-tested and set about locating them. Three-hundred-and-fifty-three people were asked to give DNA samples—all agreed and were eliminated, but there were problems locating some people. Dr. Colin Dark of the Chepstow Laboratory worked on the case for two years. He did the bulk of the work on it, which was peer-reviewed by Dr. Jonathan Whitaker. Kappen was on the list, but when police knocked on his door in August 2001, they found out that he was dead, so he slipped down the list of suspects to investigate and they continued eliminating others. In October 2001 they received DNA proof that the three rapes and murders had been committed by the same man. Police also had a major clue that would help to solve all of these crimes. Newton's body had been disposed of in a water culvert close to Garth Colliery in the village of Skewen, which was near Llandarcy. The culvert was so remote that it required local knowledge to find it. They now knew for certain that the killer was a local man and were confident that they would get him.

Whitaker suggested looking through the National DNA Database again, but this time on the assumption that the killer had criminally active offspring. He was able to produce a list of 100 profiles of people who could be the child of the killer, but one name stood out. Paul Kappen was a car-thief. They thought that it was too much of a coincidence for two members of that family to have been criminally active and for one to have been a suspect in the Llandarcy crimes, so Joseph Kappen became the main suspect. Police persuaded Kappen's widow and her daughter to give DNA samples. This enabled them to deduce an incomplete, but effective profile of Joseph Kappen by subtracting their DNA results from Paul's, which revealed the bands inherited from Joseph. The painstaking work took time, but resulted in a three quarters complete DNA profile of Joseph Kappen that matched the Llandarcy killer, even if the remaining quarter could eliminate him. There was only one way to be certain and the victims' families deserved certainty—exhume Kappen's corpse and DNA-test his remains. On December 24th, 2001 Bethell applied to the then Home Secretary, David Blunkett, for permission to exhume Kappen's remains.

Meanwhile, they researched Kappen's life and discovered that he fitted the offender profile, but there was much more besides. Kappen was an extremely vicious man who had got away with sex crimes for a decade before he became a killer. He was almost certainly a serial rapist and preyed on teenage girls, but the victims never pursued it. He thought that he was untouchable, but Bethell and his team ensured that not even death would shield him if he was, as they strongly suspected, the killer. The exhumation took place in mid-May 2002 and three weeks later the results confirmed that Joseph Kappen was the rapist and killer of Geraldine Hughes, Pauline Floyd and Sandra

Newton. The Llandarcy and Skewen files could be closed at last, but Kappen's DNA is routinely checked every six weeks against unsolved crimes. He may have been an even more prolific rapist and murderer—time will tell. Paul Bethel, his team of dogged investigators and Jonathan Whitaker, one of the top scientists of the then Forensic Science Service (FSS), all deserve great credit for unmasking Joseph Kappen as the rapist and killer that he was.

Further Resolution

That wasn't the only unsolved case in South Wales to be resolved. In December 1990, 26-year-old shipping clerk Geraldine Palk was brutally murdered. She had been stabbed 81 times, bludgeoned and raped near her home in Fairwater—a district of Cardiff while returning from a night out. Back in 1990 DNA was not ready to make a telling contribution, but that would change. A decade later the right system existed and original samples were retested and the results stored on the National DNA Database. Previous trawls of up to 4,700 local men had not yielded the desired breakthrough. It was complicated by her sexual activity that was always likely to result in a consent defence to explain traces of semen.

As Mark Hampson was nearing the end of a sentence in Dartmoor Prison for assault a random DNA sweep of inmates resulted in a match to the rape and murder of Palk. He was questioned and charged. He tried to explain the discovery of his DNA by claiming that he had had consensual sex with Palk. His claims were rejected by the jury and the trial judge, Mrs Justice (Dame Heather, now Lady Justice) Hallett, told him that he was "a vicious and violent man [with] not the slightest hint of remorse". After a renewed application for leave to appeal was dismissed Hallett decided that Hampson would have to serve a minimum term of 20 years before he would be eligible for release. However, Hampson would not serve his sentence in full—he died in prison in 2007.

The reopened investigation was led by detective chief superintendent (DCS) Wynne Phillips. Hampson was convicted in November 2002, but by then Palk's parents were dead. Her mother never came to terms with what happened to Geraldine, but Phillips, who praised the family's dignity and courage, also said that it was important for society and Geraldine's family to resolve that crime even after a decade. Phillips said that the lesson of this case is "never give up". That applies to many other cases too, as advances in forensic science, especially DNA-testing systems, mean that there is a far better chance of resolving historic unsolved cases than ever before. South Wales Police can take some credit for being ahead of the field in utilising these techniques and investigating both unsolved and unresolved homicides. Other forces should follow suit.

The Pioneering Unit

By the beginning of 1999 an important development had occurred. Forensic science caught up with the needs of samples in these cases as DNA-testing had developed into a formidable weapon in the fight against crime and equally importantly against miscarriages of justice. Another important development occurred in December 1998. The Newsagents Three (see *Chapter 1*) were freed on bail pending their appeal. Mr Justice (Sir Anthony, now Lord Justice) Hooper granted them bail, saying that the case bore all the hallmarks of a miscarriage of justice. Their appeal was set to expose the dubious methods that had been used to secure those convictions, but that had to wait until the end of the following year.

Believing that there was a serious problem and that the CJS had failed to resolve it, I joined forces with the victims of these miscarriages of justice to demand a public inquiry. It produced a stream of publicity that began to concern South Wales Police greatly. They did not want a public inquiry, naturally so if it only looked at their failings.

Renowned Cardiff solicitors Stuart Hutton and Bernard de Maid and I wrote a joint letter to the then chief constable of South Wales Police, Sir Anthony Burden, calling on him to reopen the Lynette White Inquiry. We were invited to a meeting with assistant chief constable Tony Rogers in May 1999. He told us that the Association of Chief Police Officers (ACPO) had an important policy that South Wales Police was pioneering. Following developments in forensic science they would be opening Britain's first dedicated unit to review unsolved and unresolved homicides shortly and that the Lynette White Inquiry would be the first miscarriage of justice case that they looked at. We were told that her family had already been informed and that it got a mixed response, but that they considered it essential to try to solve her murder if it was at all possible. The Major Crimes Review Unit (MCRU) came under the control of the Professional Standards Department. It would make history at the first attempt.

CHAPTER 4

THE REVIEW PROCESS

The Major Crimes Review Unit

TONY ROGERS EXPLAINED THAT FOLLOWING discussions in ACPO they had issued a new murder manual to aid investigators. This, along with developments in forensic science had convinced the force that it should establish a new unit to review unsolved and unresolved homicides. The Major Crimes Review Unit (MCRU) was the first of its kind in England and Wales; it would do just that. They had also taken advances in forensic science into account. It was less than a year since they had failed to obtain useful DNA evidence in the Lynette White Inquiry, but since then the Forensic Science Service had developed a new DNA-testing system and this would prove to have important implications for the entire CJS.

Rogers explained the procedure that the new unit would use. They would get scientific advice to decide what samples if any should be tested and what could be achieved from such testing. That involved a review of the scientific evidence, which was conducted by Dave Barclay, then Head of Physical Evidence at the National Crime and Operations Faculty (NCOF). The original investigation that resulted in the wrongful convictions of the Cardiff Three would be reviewed by retired senior officers from another force. The officers appointed for that purpose were former detective chief superintendent Bill Hacking and detective chief inspector John Thornley.

Hacking was the former head of Lancashire Police's CID. They were also tasked with ensuring that investigative opportunities that may have been missed previously would not be missed again. Rogers promised that they would be open with information as far as possible and that would include disclosure of Hacking's report when completed. In response to my question about why we should trust them, Rogers replied that I was the litmus test. They had sought their most vociferous critics and concluded that if they could convince them that they were serious and honest then they could convince anyone and in this case I was that person. Rogers wanted us to do a joint press conference, but it was too early—we had to be convinced first.

The MCRU was established in May 1999 following persistent demands for a public inquiry in South Wales. While the campaign for that inquiry was getting underway Rogers was working hard in ACPO's Homicide Working Group. Eventually the murder manual, which defined how modern murder inquiries should be investigated, was ready and the policy of establishing the MCRU was being considered. The timing of the announcement was rushed and looked like a response to the campaign for a public inquiry. But the move had in fact been considered for some time and it would now buy some time, then it had to deliver something that had never been achieved in Britain before—the resolution of a serious miscarriage of justice by convicting the real killer. If they managed that it would not only be their greatest triumph, but potentially their biggest disaster too as it would emphasise the fact that a grave miscarriage of justice had occurred.

Rogers wanted to convince critics of the force that a new dawn in policing had arrived, but that would take time and above all transparency. He gave assurances that people identified as stakeholders would be kept informed of developments, including myself. The pledges included disclosure of the Hacking Report and that he would consider giving us a copy of the murder manual as well—defence lawyers should be entitled to this as it is the standard that the police themselves believe their investigations of homicides should attain. It serves no useful purpose for this standard to be withheld from defence lawyers and the public. In fact, it suggests a conspiracy of silence where there may not be one. To date neither the murder manual nor the Hacking Report have been disclosed.

Hacking and LAGs

Former DCS Hacking and his colleague retired DCI Thornley began their review of the original Lynette White Inquiry in June 1999. There were thousands of pages of paperwork to pore over and that included my previous book. They also had to talk to several people, which included me. It was a time-consuming process. Professor Dave Barclay reviewed the scientific evidence and concluded that it did not support the police's original case hypothesis that the Cardiff Five had committed that murder and that the alleged eye-witnesses Vilday and Psaila had been forced to take part. Barclay also discovered promising leads to obtain further scientific evidence. During the course of the Hacking Review, Rogers decided to commission a Lay Advisory Group (LAG), which was supposed to consist of members of the community that would represent their interests. The idea was a good one, but it only worked if the people selected were representative of the community that they were supposed to represent and chosen by them. The first Lay Advisory Groups were established in London and the Metropolitan Police Service worked with them. It offered an opportunity to bring critics in and convince them in practice of police sincerity. It was working in London, although there were problems that ultimately succeeded in undermining LAGs.

Hacking's review of the Lynette White Inquiry was the first time a LAG was commissioned in Wales. Its terms of reference were to make recommendations, which commanded the community's respect and support, aimed at:

(a) assisting in reviewing and improving the investigation;

(b) improving the trust and confidence of the people of South Wales, particularly the diverse communities; and

(c) any other aspect of an investigation which impacts upon the community, in particular the minority ethnic community, including media communication.

The LAG's members were to be drawn from people who were:

(a) able and prepared to critically appraise police policies and practices;

(b) representative of, and commanding the respect of, the communities policed;

(c) able to make dispassionate assessments of what they experienced;

(d) committed to improving community-police relations; and

    (e)   those who could bring relevant expertise.

Serious errors were made in the way the LAG was established and how its members were chosen. Rogers asked people to serve on the LAG based on the criteria that they had set out. In my opinion this was a mistake. They should have consulted community organizations and even gone into the community and asked them to nominate their own representatives. They might have chosen some or all of the same people, but the point of LAGs was that they were supposed to be representatives of the community. Without this their conclusions would not carry the weight required. The London LAG had a document outlining its operating methods. The Cardiff one did not have such a document. It should have been agreed in advance as questions were bound to surface sooner or later.

Nevertheless, Rogers commissioned a LAG and appointed people to it. This should not have happened and certainly should not have been repeated in any other case. London's LAGs had experience and members that could provide invaluable advice to the Cardiff LAG. The rules of engagement with LAGs in other force's jurisdictions were clear. All a London LAG member was allowed to do was provide assistance and advice. They could not be a member of another LAG, let alone chair it as the point was to represent the community not tick personal boxes.

Beverley Thompson was a member of the London LAG. This was why she was approached, yet other LAG members in London were not happy as this appeared to be against their rules. The other members of the original LAG in Cardiff were David Seligman, Joy Dutfield, Norman Mills and Professor Margaret Griffiths—all of whom were known in Cardiff, but were they representative of the community in Butetown? Community representatives such as Betty Campbell were not approached and there was no attempt to establish who the community trusted and wanted as their representatives. This would become an ongoing concern as other LAGs in South Wales followed the same pattern of appointment for the community rather than selection by it.

The local members of the Cardiff LAG were keen to serve, open and their approach was refreshing. I tried to raise the London issue but Thompson said that this had to be done in London. My view was that that LAGs were supposed to provide a bridge between local communities and the police. They are part of a policy of open policing and can only work if they have the support of the community that they are supposed to represent.

The other members explained their credentials and how they came to be members of the LAG and why they accepted the invitation. Mills said that he was proud to be asked to serve. They even said that they hoped I got the answers that I was looking for and recognised my concerns, trying to answer them as best they could. Thompson later left the Cardiff LAG and Professor Griffiths took over as chair. The constitution of the Cardiff LAG still lacked true democratic input and consultation with the local community, and questions remain over how the representatives came to be appointed.

The LAG saw all the evidence that Hacking reviewed and both Hacking and Thornley kept them informed of developments throughout their review. One of my questions to Thompson proved to be prophetic. If there is a conflict between the police's desire for confidentiality and the community's wish to know, which would she favour? I got no answer at the meeting—so I reciprocated by ignoring demands addressed to me. After all, I knew a lot about this case but I felt that there should have been greater openness.

On September 8th 2000, Hacking's review was completed and Tony Rogers decided that after all he would not disclose it to the identified stakeholders. He explained why in advance of the press conference that he called to discuss Hacking's review and the way forward and we accepted his reasons.

Warts and All

The second phase of the investigation (Hacking's review had been the first) would go down in history as one of the best investigations of all time, but before it reached its triumphant conclusion there was a lot of painstaking research and investigation to be conducted. The LAG pronounced itself satisfied that the review had been conducted thoroughly and honestly. It almost certainly was. Rogers believed that Hacking's review had revealed new lines of inquiry that could lead to the crime being solved, using the rather euphemistic phrase that "there were warts in the original inquiry". They would return to this later, but how open and honest was the review and subsequent investigation? Both made history and they plainly did not sweep inconvenient evidence under the carpet, but final judgement on the Hacking Review cannot be passed until it is disclosed. The leads that Hacking discovered—whatever they happened to be—were not the ones that led to the resolution of the Lynette White Inquiry.

A team of 16 officers, led by detective superintendent Kevin O'Neill were appointed to investigate the murder of Lynette White. Hacking was retained as a consultant. Resources were made available for DNA-testing as well. Rogers was determined to solve the murder of Lynette White and nothing would be allowed to interfere with that objective. Despite the need to protect the integrity of evidence and lines of inquiry, it is essential that it does not become a permanent excuse for not disclosing Hacking's report. Rogers suggested asking the LAG to raise the issue periodically, but the question of disclosure of that report was soon overtaken by more important events. O'Neill and his team had history to make.

CHAPTER 5

COMMITTED — THE INVESTIGATION AFTER HACKING

Broken Promises

THE HACKING REVIEW HAD TAKEN 15 months, considerably longer than expected. A press conference was called to announce Hacking's findings and to inform the assembled throng of journalists what would happen next. Rogers said that he knew that he was going to have to take some hits for going back on his promise of disclosure, but explained the reasons for his decision. The review had discovered lines of inquiry that he believed could help to solve the murder and that was his force's priority. Disclosure might compromise that. It was understandable, although I felt that the report could have been disclosed with an undertaking of confidentiality. Nevertheless, I also appreciated their desire to ensure that vital information could not get into the public domain. The LAG had been kept fully informed of all developments rapidly and had seen the relevant materials. They attended the press conference and pronounced themselves satisfied that the review had been conducted thoroughly, efficiently and honestly.

Although there were sound reasons to withhold disclosure, non-disclosure offers a fertile breeding ground for conspiracy theories whether there is a conspiracy or not. It is one of the reasons why the Hacking Report must be disclosed as soon as possible and South Wales Police should publicly commit themselves to do so as soon as it becomes feasible, but even if they originally thought that the Cardiff Five were guilty the evidence would soon put them straight if they were honest enough to follow it wherever it led them. Their preconceptions mattered less than their investigative integrity. They could think what they wanted as long as they gathered evidence honestly and allowed it to speak unfettered by their opinions. They may well have done so, but only full disclosure can prove it beyond doubt. However,

Hacking's report and recommendations have still not been made public, so judgement has to be reserved.

According to a reliable source, the original aims of reopening the case were to prove that, while the rules had been bent, the Cardiff Five were still somehow involved in the murder. Until the report and investigation is published it is impossible to judge if those claims are true or not, but it still has to be taken seriously. Sir Anthony Burden said that Hacking's review had scrutinised the procedures used in the original investigation and made 107 recommendations, relating to the investigative processes and procedures in the original investigation. The recommendations were designed to improve investigative and procedural techniques in future inquiries. Burden said that some of those recommendations had already been implemented before the review and that others would be carried out. Over a decade later it remains unknown if this has happened yet or will happen soon. South Wales Police should consider whether the recommendations that Hacking made can be disclosed without prejudicing any current developments in relation to the case.[1] Otherwise, there is a danger that by the time they are disclosed they will already be out of date. Rogers revealed that Hacking's review had discovered lines of inquiry that he believed had to be investigated.

The Lynette White Inquiry was formally re-opened in September 2000. Hacking was instructed as a consultant to the reinvestigation and Rogers appointed a team of 16 police officers to the inquiry. He promised that resources would be made available for DNA-testing and kept his word. There were another eight unsolved homicides to be considered. They promised that all of them would all be reviewed and the second was already underway — the murders of Harry and Megan Tooze. The reviewing officer for that case, which had previously resulted in the wrongful conviction of Jonathan Jones, was Malcolm Ross, recently retired detective superintendent of West Midlands Police.

The pattern of investigations had been set, or so it seemed. There was another murder inquiry that was very significant. It forced itself onto the

---

1. Those proceedings have ended but the case is still subject to procedures. The trial of eight police officers and two witnesses for conspiracy to pervert the course of justice and perjury ended with their being acquitted on December 1st, 2011: see *Chapter 13*. There is thus in my view no basis for not immediately releasing the Hacking Report, or its recommendations.

agenda without being reviewed and that would later cause problems. Despite following the Lynette White Inquiry into history, the Karen Skipper Inquiry would make unwanted history as well, but that was many years away and would make its mark without being looked at by the MCRU at all. Meanwhile, the Lynette White Inquiry was ready to move to the next stage, but first there was an obstacle to overcome. Memories were long and forgiveness in short supply. Trust would have to be regained and that meant it had to be earned by actions.

Regaining Trust

It was time for the new team of investigators and forensic scientists to prove their mettle. Detective superintendent Kevin O'Neill was in charge of the reopened inquiry and Brent Parry was the senior investigating officer in day-to-day charge of the investigation. For all their faults in the original investigation police and scientists unwittingly ensured that the same force would get a second chance to put right their mistakes and forensic science would be at the heart of it. The Cardiff Five should have been eliminated on the basis of blood grouping and DNA. Sadly that did not happen and an implausible cocktail hypothesis was presented to the jury in the 1990 trial. Nevertheless, O'Neill knew that he had cause to be grateful to the original investigators and scientists, because they packaged and stored items very well. That made it possible to locate those items and subject them to modern DNA-tests, as advances in forensic science had given them the means to secure vital evidence to tie the real killer to his crime, but they also knew that other possible sources of foreign DNA had to be located before testing could prove as useful as it could be.

O'Neill and his team knew that mistakes had been made in the original investigation and that their investigation would be closely scrutinised. They had to present everything to the Lay Advisory Group and some observers were biding their time — waiting for them to fall flat on their faces, at which point they would pounce. Consequently, they knew that the stakes were high. After deciding to withhold the Hacking Report in order to try to solve the murder, they desperately needed a result, but this time it had to be the right one. A second miscarriage of justice would not be tolerated, and patience would not last for ever. They were under serious pressure. South Wales Police had been given a chance to put things right, but this time they had to make history by finding the real killer.

The original investigation had eroded a lot of trust especially in what remained of the once vibrant community that Butetown had been. Its soul had been developed out of existence, but memories were long and there were people who remembered the case and how Butetown had been vilified by the police well. While everybody wanted to see the real killer brought to justice, few in that community trusted the police to put things right. Nevertheless, hostilities were put on hold while they were given a chance to prove that they were serious about solving it correctly. It was up to them to take it, but as far as trust in the community went, they would have to earn it back. That was one of the unfortunate legacies that they faced. They were judged — unfairly — by the sins of the previous investigation, but they remained determined to prove their trustworthiness by solving Lynette's murder against the odds. It was a difficult task, but one that was necessary to right the wrongs of the past and to convince their many critics that the force had changed.

Phase Two

O'Neill and Parry were a formidable pair who inspired their team through the disappointing times when it appeared that the case would defy their attempts to solve it, but they persevered. They faced disapproval from colleagues who believed that they should let sleeping dogs lie. They were on a hiding to nothing and they knew it, but they continued investigating tenaciously. If they succeeded in solving Lynette's murder they would make history: a fantastic investigation that would succeed in resolving a miscarriage of justice with the conviction of the truly guilty killer. But this would would also prove beyond doubt that the Cardiff Five were, as they always insisted, completely innocent and this would lead to awkward questions about the original investigation. It would pit modernising honest police officers against historic investigations and methods that that could never have been justified. This would require courage and integrity and plenty of it. It was the most important test of South Wales Police's integrity ever.

They investigated several lines of inquiry, but recognised quickly that forensic science would be the key. Dave Barclay had already reviewed the scientific evidence and established that there were opportunities to obtain important scientific evidence that could be used against the real killer. Police had also consulted behavioural analysts in the USA. They investigated the possibility of wound analysis as the National Crimes and Operations Faculty (NCOF) operated an injuries database, but this was not followed up. Barclay's analysis was crucial, not only in setting the Lynette White Inquiry back on an even keel, but in helping to solve her brutal murder. Barclay quickly concluded that in his opinion scientific evidence had been misinterpreted in the original investigation by Dr. Peter Gill and also by Dr. John Whiteside. Gill's Y-chromosome analysis established that the murderer was male, but Gill wavered in his conclusions. This allowed Whiteside to offer a fanciful explanation for the foreign blood that was discovered in the flat.

Whiteside claimed that it could have been a mixture of Psaila's blood with that of an unknown male. At the first trial it was suggested by David Elfer QC that the man in question was Abdullahi. A DNA-test proved that it wasn't. There never was any evidence that proved Whiteside's "cocktail hypothesis" to be true and the scenario of a male killer acting on his own was never conclusively eliminated. Whiteside's hypothesis was extremely unlikely as it required not only a thorough mix from a split second contact, but for that mixture to land next to Lynette's blood. It was therefore not just a mixture of Psaila's blood with an unknown male killer, but with Lynette's as well. A cocktail of two people's blood mixing intimately from a split second contact was highly implausible. Unfortunately the jury never heard that Whiteside's claims were even more questionable — after mixing intimately from such contact this cocktail of blood just happened to land right next to a blood-stain deposited by Lynette to create a three person cocktail. It stretched credibility to breaking point.

Barclay's research established that the scientific evidence did not support the Crown's original hypothesis of five killers acting in tandem, along with two coerced witnesses. He reviewed the scene of crime photographs carefully and noticed that one of the many stains on the wall near to the corner of the room where Lynette died was likely to have dripped down the wall. The trail of blood that it belonged to had got stronger the further one moved from Lynette's body. It couldn't have been shed by Lynette. Barclay therefore recommended that the skirting board and the paint be carefully removed—the flat had been painted over in 1988 because it was a health hazard. It proved to be a blessing as it sealed the killer's blood in until forensic science was ready to reveal its grisly secret.

The door to and wallpaper from the flat was removed, and the flat carefully reconstructed by the police in their headquarters. It was a stroke of genius as it enabled Barclay to reconstruct the exit route of the killer from the flat. The crime occurred in the dead of night and there was no lighting, so Barclay wore a blindfold and went through the flat. Every place that he touched with his right hand was diligently noted. This method established not only where the killer had touched—eventually yielding precious DNA profiles of the murderer—but his height too from the position of the stains. Barclay stood six foot tall and it was concluded that the killer would be slightly shorter than him; he was right. The paint was removed with great care and attention to prevent the destruction of evidence and blood was discovered in those positions. These items were DNA-tested and found to belong to the killer. It was already known that the killer had cut his hand and that some of the blood-staining on the bottom of Lynette's jeans and her left sock had been deposited by the killer. Both yielded full DNA profiles, which meant that O'Neill's team had the killer's DNA on record.

The scene of crime photos also revealed a tantalising piece of evidence. There was blood-staining on the inside of the front door of 7 James Street. Lynette could not have deposited that blood there as she was already dead. It had to have been deposited by the real killer or someone that had been in the flat, discovered the body and fled. Police knew its significance immediately, but in 1988 it was too small to tell its story. Conventional blood grouping tests were not conducted on it back then, but everyone knew that it had an important tale to tell without the means to do so. It had to wait over a decade to reveal the evidence it had held for so long. Forensic science would play a very important role in this investigation, but it was far from the only line of inquiry. Hacking's review had identified leads that needed to be investigated. People of interest had to be traced, interviewed and eliminated. That applied to suspects too. Fingerprint evidence was revisited as well. Operation Mistral had history to make and O'Neill and Parry were absolutely determined that it would.

It involved a long and painstaking review of every exhibit in the police's possession to identify opportunities to locate the DNA of the killer and much more besides. That required extraordinary patience and commitment of resources by South Wales Police to identify potential locations of the DNA of the killer and the funds to conduct these tests. It also required some fantastic work by forensic scientists to locate sources of DNA, extract them and test them. This evidence would make another miscarriage of justice impossible, as suspects' DNA profiles could be compared to that of the killer and they would be eliminated if it didn't match. Rogers would prove to be a man of his word. He promised that funds would be made available for DNA-testing and they were. It was crucial both in regaining public trust and in solving a very difficult case — one that provided valuable lessons not only for the police, but also people protesting their innocence.

CHAPTER 6

THE SCIENTIFIC EVIDENCE

An Integrated Approach

THE MURDER OF LYNETTE WHITE required the modern DNA-testing system to obtain the evidence to solve it, but it also needed an integrated approach to the use of forensic science. Even though DNA played a quite important part in resolving the miscarriage of justice that befell the Cardiff Five by helping to convict the real killer, it should not be forgotten that it required other scientific techniques in order to shine. The police had an obvious starting point to get the DNA profile of the killer, but they needed more evidence and they knew it. The previous miscarriage of justice meant that they had to prove their case every step of the way, as any doubt would be exploited by a stark warning: "We don't want another Cardiff Five do we?"

Professor Barclay's review of the scientific evidence helped to establish that the police were looking for a killer acting on his own, as the scientific evidence did not support the original case scenario that the Cardiff Five had committed the murder along with two frightened alleged eye-witnesses. The police had also sought advice from behavioural analysts in the USA, which confirmed that the murderer was likely to be Caucasian, or Asian, a punter and had acted alone. It wasn't unexpected, but confirmed Barclay's interpretation of the scientific evidence and helped to convince O'Neill and his team that they were looking for one killer acting on his own. The NCOF also ran the fledgling National Injuries Database (NIB), which kept records of injuries inflicted in numerous crimes. The pattern of injuries could have revealed links to other crimes. Despite initial contact, the NIB was not consulted in the end. It was a possible line of inquiry that may have broadened the scope of the investigation, but they had a scientific trump card — they had the DNA profile of the killer. There wasn't much DNA left from the bloodstains on Lynette's jeans and sock that could not have been shed by Lynette.

Nevertheless, the new system did not require much material to yield useful results. Full DNA profiles (ten genes and the test for the Y-chromosome) were obtained from both samples. They could now concentrate on trying to locate more DNA of the killer to compliment the picture that was beginning to emerge.

Independence and Verification

The DNA-testing system that would prove vital in solving the murder of Lynette White was developed by the Forensic Science Service (FSS). During the original investigation the FSS had a monopoly and worked exclusively for the police. Both Whiteside and Gill worked at FSS laboratories. The manipulation of the scientific evidence in the original case counted against the FSS and this was unfortunate as the scientists that developed SGM+ had done nothing wrong. Nevertheless, forensic scientists who worked for the FSS had been involved in some major miscarriages of justice — Frank Skuse's involvement in the case of Hugh Callaghan, Paddy Hill, Gerry Hunter, Richard McIlkenny, Billy Power and Johnny Walker (the Birmingham Six) became a cause célèbre. Judith Ward also suffered a major miscarriage of justice due to manipulation of scientific evidence. Ronald Outteridge was fortunate not to face trial over his role in the tragic case of Stefan Kiszko, which would later result in posthumous vindication with the conviction of Ronald Castree in 2007, and there were plenty more too.[1]

Forensic science was opened up to competition in the 1990s, which resulted in the FSS losing its monopoly over work for the police and suffering from the perception that it was biased in favour of them, which cost it work from defendants. Its previous record in the Lynette White Inquiry also convinced Rogers that it would be best not to use the FSS. That was Forensic Alliance's opportunity and Angela Gallup seized it. I suggested that it would be beneficial to have the scientific evidence verified by an independent laboratory that had no connection to the original investigation, Home

---

1. Stefan Kiszko served 16 years for the 1975 murder of Lesley Moleseed: a crime he definitely did not commit and for which another man was later convicted, see *Chapter 12* of this work.

Office or FSS, as that would verify the bona fides of the scientific evidence in circumstances where the previous history of the case could have muddied the waters. I recommended Professor Bernd Brinkmann's Instituts für Rechtsmedizin at the University of Münster in northern Germany and Rogers readily agreed. Dr. Stephen Rand undertook the task, but eventually concluded that the work of Forensic Alliance did not need to be reviewed.

DNA

Kevin O'Neill's team painstakingly reviewed every item that was in the possession of the police from the original inquiry to establish opportunities to locate DNA that could prove useful. Investigations established that several items that had been packaged and stored by South Wales Police without being tested in 1988 were blood-stained and may have been worthwhile evidence. Numerous items were tested and not all of them yielded useful results, but some did. A piece of cellophane wrapping from a cigarette packet had blood on it, so it was DNA-tested and it matched the profile of the killer. The smear on the inside of the communal door to 7 James Street that was of great interest previously, but too small for conventional blood grouping tests, was sent for DNA-testing. It yielded the same profile that had been obtained from the piece of cellophane. The killer was nick-named "Cellophane Man" because that DNA profile was also found on a blood-stained piece of cellophane. A cardboard box was also blood-stained and it too yielded a DNA profile that matched Cellophane Man. These results were certainly useful, but they were not enough to prove guilt.

Due to the previous miscarriage of justice some people still did not trust South Wales Police to resolve the Lynette White Inquiry correctly. They need not have worried. The scene of crime photographs proved that the blood had been deposited on these items in 1988. What on earth was the point of planting blood in 1988, ignoring it then and allowing a notorious miscarriage of justice to occur, only to return to the original scapegoat 15 years afterwards? All that would do is expose the original miscarriage of justice for what it was. It made no sense at all. If that blood had been planted, then the police would have framed the person it belonged to in 1988. There was another huge problem with the planting accusation. If they were going to plant someone's blood at this crime scene, such an attempt would be exposed by blood distribution analysis, but even more importantly, surely they would know whose blood it was. The killer was known as Cellophane Man for a reason — they had no idea who he was. The suggestion that this blood was planted is preposterous and there was further evidence that would prove beyond doubt that it could not have been planted.

Barclay's review had identified several avenues of investigation during the Hacking Review (*Chapter 5*) that would prove vital later. He recommended removing a piece of skirting board, because he noticed that one drip of blood on the wall could not have been shed by Lynette. It was part of a trail that got stronger as you moved away from the body. Had it been Lynette's it would have got weaker. He believed that this particular stain would have dripped down the wall to the skirting board and would have been sealed in by the paint. Angela Gallup who worked for Forensic Alliance found that blood had seeped into the gap between the skirting board and the wall. It was extracted and DNA-tested. It matched Cellophane Man.

While there was the opportunity — however ludicrous the scenario — to plant the blood on the items that had been recovered by police during the original investigation, the skirting board and wall had been painted over as a health hazard in 1988 and the blood sealed in. It was nonsensical to suggest that that blood had been planted and for the DNA profile of it to have knowingly matched Cellophane Man then for entirely different suspects to been arrested and without any reference to it. DNA profiles matching Cellophane Man were also obtained from a cardboard box and other items of Lynette's clothing, but the investigators were still not satisfied.

There was more DNA to obtain from under other paintwork as noted in *Chapter 5*. Barclay had also reconstructed the exit route of the killer from the living room and through the hall to the stairway by going through the flat blindfolded. Every place that he touched with his right hand was carefully noted. The paint was carefully removed and the blood that had been sealed in, and as it turned out preserved by the paint, was extracted with great attention to detail. Gallup's team did not want to damage the blood and consequently the DNA. Blood was extracted from the walls in the living room and hall and on the inside of the door to Flat 1, 7 James Street, as a result of Barclay's reconstruction. Full DNA profiles were obtained from these samples and they matched that of Cellophane Man.

Incredibly the significance of Barclay's achievement has not been properly appreciated. Police forces share information, so all forces know that it is possible in certain circumstances to reconstruct the exit route of murderers if crimes were committed indoors and the murderer had cut himself. It won't apply in every case, but it is astonishing that no prisoner protesting his or her innocence or lawyer representing people in such cases has realised that Barclay's reconstruction technique may prove useful in their cases. Barclay proved that it was possible over a decade later to reconstruct the exit route of a murderer who had cut his hand and Angela Gallup proved that certain types of paint not only do not inhibit obtaining DNA profiles but preserve the DNA for years. This information should have pricked up the ears of both those protesting innocence and their legal representatives. In fact, they should study Operation Mistral (i.e. this investigation) carefully in terms of how sources of new evidence were located and obtained—it is a model of how to use modern investigative techniques in difficult cases.

It had taken several months to locate these sources of DNA, test them and discover that they all originated from Cellophane Man. This was powerful evidence. The blood-stains discovered by Barclay's reconstruction could not have been planted by O'Neill's team or the forensic scientists who worked on the reopened investigation as they did not have access to the flat in 1988—the latest that the blood could have been put there. That meant that if anyone had planted Gafoor's blood at the crime-scene it had to have been done in 1988, so it could only have been done by the police who investigated the murder originally or by forensic scientists. Why would they take the trouble to plant blood and allow it to be painted over? Even more importantly, what would be the point of planting blood at a crime-scene and then arresting and charging different people, whose combination of blood groups was vastly different? If it had been planted, they must have known whose blood it was and that it was therefore likely to undermine the prosecution of the Cardiff Five. Planting that blood was not possible or plausible.

For all their faults, there is no way that they would have arrested and charged the wrong people if they had known who had deposited that foreign blood in Flat 1, 7 James Street, as that made no sense at all and there is another problem with such accusations against the original investigators. Jeffrey Gafoor was not known to the police in 1988. He had no criminal record at all at that time. There was no record of Gafoor coming to the attention of the police during the original inquiry, so how could they have had access to his blood and why would they choose him as the scapegoat for this crime? It would require great skill to solve the murder of Lynette White correctly.

Closing in on the Killer

It had taken 15 months to locate and extract material and then obtain DNA profiles from all of these items. In January 2002 O'Neill decided to up the ante. They announced that they had the DNA profile of a man that they believed was involved in the murder of Lynette White and appealed to the public for help. They wanted to conduct a mass DNA screening in the area, partly in the hope of getting lucky and finding out who Cellophane Man was, but also to increase pressure on him. They believed that someone close to him knew what he had done and wanted that person to come forward and help them.

The mass screening began. It included suspects and people of interest. At first it targeted known people. They intended to DNA-test up to 5,000 people. The public was told that DNA profiles had been obtained from men and women from the crime scene, but that one was of particular interest as it belonged to a man that the police believed was directly involved in the murder. They intended to conduct an intelligence-led DNA sweep of the local area. Assistant chief constable Rogers said that O'Neill's team, which was now 20 strong, would be increased if required. They appealed for people to volunteer their DNA and many did, but the process needed public support and the police had a novel way of getting it. They would find the people who have least reason of all to trust or help them and ask for their support publicly by taking a DNA-test. Well there was no doubt who those people were—the Cardiff Five.

Proved Innocent

They had no reason at all to trust the police, but these were positive developments. DNA could prove them innocent beyond doubt and they could encourage others to take the test. If they agreed to be DNA-tested after all that had happened to them how could others refuse? The police approached their lawyers who were hesitant, but who also asked my advice. I told them that they had nothing to fear from the DNA-tests—it would unequivocally clear them as it was impossible for their DNA to match that of Cellophane Man when their combination of blood groups didn't, but before they would cooperate some safeguards had to be agreed. The Cardiff Five would not be arrested. They would not give samples in a police station. Police would come to them. It was agreed that the police would attend their solicitors' offices. The media would be invited to record the sample being taken. The samples would be sealed and signed in their presence and that of their legal representative. The lawyer would then accompany police taking the samples to the testing laboratory and witness it being stored pending testing. They could attend both the testing and the destruction of excess DNA as well if they wished to. Tony Paris was the first to volunteer his DNA, which was done in the office of his solicitor Marilyn Bishop. They even objected to the two officers that were due to take the samples and they were replaced. The reason for the objection was that those officers were involved in the controversial case of the Merthyr Two[2] and Paris did not feel comfortable giving his DNA to them.

The police agreed to all the terms requested by Paris' legal team. All of the Cardiff Five agreed to be tested, but Paris was first. He chose not to permit his DNA or data to be stored on the National DNA Database. He then told the assembled media that he was glad to have the opportunity to prove his innocence and asked the public to cooperate with the DNA screening process. In March 2002 the first results were revealed. Paris' DNA had not been discovered in 7 James Street and nor had Yusef Abdullahi's. They had just been proven innocent. Later Stephen Miller, John Actie and Ronnie Actie

---

2. Annette Hewins and Donna Clarke: see the Gurnos Estate arson case mentioned in *Chapter 1* and *Appendix 2*.

were also proved innocent. "I'm happy for my community, for my family and everybody else," said Paris. "I knew I wasn't involved and I was glad to have the opportunity to prove it."

It is astonishing that others in the same position as Paris seem unaware of the safeguards that were agreed to by South Wales Police to be allowed to get his DNA. This should be a blueprint to ensure that people such as Paris who have no reason to trust the police agree to cooperate. It is also in the best interests of the police as by doing it in public with such safeguards they are protected from spurious accusations of malpractice. Meanwhile, the police continued the laborious task of working through the 5,000 people who had been involved in the original inquiry and there was no guarantee that the killer would be one of them. Nevertheless, police were determined to identify Lynette's killer and would continue the search until they found him.

CHAPTER 7

IDENTIFYING THE KILLER AND THE IMPLICATIONS

The Sweep

ASSISTANT CHIEF CONSTABLE ROGERS HAD announced that police had the DNA profile of a man that they were particularly interested in. They believed that Cellophane Man was directly involved in the murder, but they also wanted to trace and eliminate both men and women whose DNA had been discovered in the flat, but were not involved in the murder. They began an intelligence-led DNA screening exercise of 5,000 people who were involved in the original investigation. The Cardiff Five were the first to be eliminated as the source of the DNA deposited in the flat. None of them was Cellophane Man. They had been wrongly stigmatised for many highly damaging years. A public apology was the very least that they deserved, but that would come later.

Meanwhile, the police continued the screening process, which was time-consuming. Months passed. They checked the National DNA Database, but Cellophane Man's DNA was not on it, which was a huge surprise and challenged many assumptions. It was possible that the killer had emigrated and continued his criminal activities abroad, but despite having the DNA of the killer it is harder to check international DNA databases than it should be. Police can ask Interpol (the International Criminal Police Organization) to ask member organizations if there are any similar crimes in other jurisdictions, but while offender behaviour may have unique features that can link crimes, DNA is a different matter.

Many jurisdictions use SGM+,[1] but the USA does not. CODIS (Combined DNA Index System) is a database run by the FBI, but it only shares seven of the ten genes that SGM+ uses, even though CODIS tests at 13 genes. It is not

---

1. SGM stands for Second Generation Multiplex.

difficult to run the relevant DNA-test, but the problems are more likely to be legal ones. Different jurisdictions have their own legal requirements and in some of them even convicted killers cannot be compelled to give samples for DNA-testing, which makes it difficult to compare DNA results except at the genes that are shared by the different DNA-testing systems.

There were no guarantees that the killer had remained in Britain, but as with the previous investigation police concentrated on Britain, especially South Wales. Their intelligence-led screening process succeeded in eliminating several people, but it failed to identify Cellophane Man. Months passed. The decision to try to increase the pressure on the killer seemed to have backfired and the public's patience was running out.

Inspired

Obtaining the DNA profile of Cellophane Man was obviously a significant breakthrough, but he was proving incredibly difficult to identify. He was not on the National DNA Database, which meant that he had not been arrested for a violent crime since the database was established in the mid-1990s, which was very surprising. Was he dead, or had he emigrated? Police continued to believe that he was in Britain. In fact they thought that he hadn't strayed far from his base in South Wales. So far the screening process had failed to identify him and no relative or friend had come forward to put a name to him. Was he ever going to be found?

During Operation Mistral another case that was to play an important role in solving this case occurred. As mentioned in *Chapter 2*, Joseph Kappen was exposed as a cowardly killer. Kappen had raped and murdered three 16-year-old girls in 1973. He died in 1990, so his DNA and data have not been stored on the National DNA Database. The forensic scientist Jonathan Whitaker had the idea of checking the database for the DNA of a child of the Llandarcy killer. Paul Kappen's stood out — he was Joseph's son. With the aid of Kappen's ex-wife and daughter they were able to deduce three-quarters of Joseph Kappen's DNA profile. It was enough to secure an exhumation order. DNA was taken from Kappen's corpse and tested by Colin Dark. It proved that Kappen was indeed the Llandarcy serial killer.

Could it possibly work again? Detective constable Paul Williams was determined to find out. One allele (or band) out of the 20 in the DNA profile of the killer was very rare. Ninety-nine per cent of the people whose data was stored on the database could be eliminated on the basis of that allele alone. A DNA expert, Andrew MacDonald, suggested looking for a familial link, starting with the rare allele. Williams assisted. He began by searching for just seven allele positions. The initial search gave 600 hits. He then applied it to people from South Wales and increased the parameters to 12 alleles from the profile of Cellophane Man, which produced 70 matches, but one result stood out — a 14-year-old criminally active boy, who was a close relative of Cellophane Man. That profile was so close to that of Cellophane Man that the police knew this was a significant development. They now knew the family that Cellophane Man belonged to — he was a close relative of that teenage boy. Williams was now convinced that they would soon have their man and he was right.

Jeffrey Gafoor was a 37-year-old security guard. He had two brothers including the father of the criminally active boy. The police set about getting DNA samples from male members of that family. The boy's father was tested and eliminated. An uncle was tested and cleared as well. Police were puzzled now. The DNA told them the killer was a close male relative of that boy, but the results told them that it wasn't his father or uncle. They didn't know of any other close relatives, so they went back to the family and were told that there was another uncle — Jeffrey Gafoor — who had chosen to live a reclusive life and cut himself off from the family. They didn't know why. That mystery would soon be solved and Gafoor would be revealed as one of Britain's most frightening killers, because he was so difficult to detect, despite leaving several clues. He was scary because he was so ordinary — the last person that would have been suspected.

Police visited Gafoor and requested a sample for DNA-testing. If he refused they had no power to force him to assist unless they arrested him, although refusal would have raised their suspicions. When told that it was regarding the Lynette White Inquiry, the killer's response was telling. "Haven't you got someone for that?" he said. It proved that Gafoor knew that innocent men had suffered for his crime — he didn't care at the time or now. He tried to explain away the inexplicable without raising suspicion, or so he thought — instead he was removing doubt that police had their man, but they still needed his DNA. Realising that his DNA was at the crime scene, he made another important remark. He asked if it was from semen and told them that he had had sex with Lynette a week before she was murdered. If that was meant to throw police off the trail it had the opposite effect — the DNA had not come from semen and it was obvious that Gafoor was trying to give an innocent explanation for his DNA being at the crime scene. Williams knew that he was face-to-face with the killer. He asked for a mouth swab for DNA-testing. Incredibly, Gafoor agreed and provided the sample. It was sent to Forensic Alliance and fast-tracked. He was now the prime suspect and put under secret surveillance while they waited for the results. Could they finally put a name to Cellophane Man? It was February 27th 2003 — Gafoor's last day of freedom, but it could have been so different.

The Case for a Complete DNA Database

O'Neill and his team were all but certain that Cellophane Man had been unmasked as 37-year-old security guard Jeffrey Gafoor. They would soon be proved right, but what would have happened if Gafoor's nephew had been a law-abiding individual and had thus not been on the National DNA Database, or Gafoor had declined to give a sample for DNA-testing? It almost doesn't bear thinking about. With what we know of Gafoor's character traits and behaviour after the murder it is unlikely that he would have committed an offence that allowed police access to his DNA and if his relatives had also avoided contact with police, solving Lynette's murder would have been impossible without a great deal of luck. Is it acceptable that resolving a notorious miscarriage of justice with the conviction of the truly guilty depended on luck? His nephew's DNA information being on the database was the crucial piece of luck that police needed. If that had not happened, Gafoor would not have been brought to justice and the Cardiff Five would still be enduring a thoroughly unjustified whispering campaign. That would have been yet another injustice. So how can the need for luck to solve such cases have been eliminated then and in the future? The obvious answer is a complete National DNA Database and it would help to prevent miscarriages of justice before they happened as well. If every person's DNA, or at least a record of their profiles was on it, Gafoor would have been identified as a suspect as soon as the profiles of Cellophane Man were obtained.

The National DNA Database has helped to solve thousands of crimes, including murder and rape. DNA databasing is a very valuable tool not just in fighting crime, but also in preventing it. It has also helped to prevent miscarriages of justice and will do so again. If a crime like Lynette White's murder were to occur today with a comprehensive database, not only would Gafoor be identified quickly, but innocent people would have been able to prove their innocence rapidly. A complete DNA Database is therefore an important weapon in proving innocence and would benefit "the usual suspects" greatly if they were in fact innocent. I used to oppose such a database passionately, but the hunt for Cellophane Man helped to change my mind.

Nothing can justify the whispering campaign that damaged the Cardiff Five for over a decade. They can't get those years back or have the damage they suffered undone, but the lessons can and must be learned. I support a fully independent national DNA database that would contain at least the records of the DNA profiles of every citizen. However, I have always been unequivocally opposed to the records, DNA profiles and excess DNA being held or controlled by the police or any other agency of the state, but it should however be noted that the police have never had control of the database.

The judgement in the European Court of Human Rights in *S and Michael Marper v UK*[2] forbids the retention of DNA information of people who have not been convicted of any offence in Wales and England. The former government's response was to draft legislation that allowed them to continue to do that for a limited period. Despite this, I believe there should be a fully independent DNA database of every male and female of every racial origin, but only with carefully defined and effective safeguards to prevent abuse—and that must be achieved through consent, not compulsion. It is still possible to achieve this, but an informed debate is urgent. No actual DNA is stored on the database, just the electronic profile of a small non-coding area. This means that there are no commercial implications. For example, there should be no concern about the database being used for further analysis of the material

---

2. See http://www.bailii.org/eu/cases/ECHR/2008/1581.html

to determine the genetic probabilities of developing diseases, which could be used by insurance companies.

The police should be nothing more than clients of such a database, but so should defence lawyers. The police don't need any greater powers and it seems that a police-based system would not enjoy public trust. The database must only be controlled by a fully independent body and it must be protected by stringent safeguards to prevent abuse. The police should not even collect samples from individuals or supply them to the database—that should be done by staff or accredited agents of the fully independent DNA database. The police would ask the custodians of the database to check crime scene results to identify possible lines of inquiry and any results should be disclosed to defence lawyers, who should have the right to hire forensic scientists to investigate further. We can only guess at how many other miscarriages of justice could be corrected, or better still prevented entirely, if there was a complete and independent national DNA database. Equally important, we can only wonder how many unsolved crimes could be resolved quickly. Some miscarriages of justice could also be resolved with the conviction of the truly guilty. So why hasn't this debate been started, let alone concluded?

The Identification of Cellophane Man and its Implications

Paul Williams was one of the officers to obtain a mouth swab from Gafoor on February 27th 2003. Within a day police had the response they had been hoping for. The net had all but closed on the new prime suspect. Jeffrey Gafoor was Cellophane Man, which was confirmed by Forensic Alliance, but there were still further dramas to unfold before Gafoor was brought to justice. It was, however, a good job that the police had put him under surveillance, as even at this late stage in proceedings Gafoor wanted to cheat justice—he would try to overdose on paracetamol, but his life would be saved by the police, who were determined to see him answer for his crime. Like it or not Gafoor was going to have to face justice, but there were important lessons from the way that he was unmasked that need to be understood and utilised in other cases. The inquiry into the Llandarcy rapes and murders that had been so ably led by Paul Bethell had pioneered the use of familial DNA to help to identify killers who were not on the National DNA Database. Joseph Kappen was dead, but his family was alive and his son Paul's DNA was on the database. The DNA of Kappen's ex-wife, her daughter and Paul Kappen helped to isolate enough to build a 15 allele DNA profile of Joseph Kappen. It matched the crime scene DNA at all 15 alleles, but police needed to know the other five to either eliminate Kappen or tie him conclusively to the crimes. The 15 allele DNA profile was enough to secure an exhumation order that enabled them to obtain a full DNA profile from Kappen's corpse, which proved that he was a vicious killer.

A variation of these methods was used by Paul Williams in the Lynette White Inquiry, which showed that it was possible to solve crimes even if you did not have a direct hit from the National DNA Database. In both cases the real killer's DNA was not on the database, but rather than wait and hope for the killer to commit a crime that would allow his DNA to be taken and tested and compared to unsolved crimes—impossible in Kappen's case for obvious reasons—they decided to take a proactive approach and investigate further. In both cases the investigators assumed that the tendency to commit crimes might run in the family. They had the DNA of the killer, but they didn't know who it belonged to, but they knew that in both cases the killer's DNA was not on the database. Bethell and Williams showed that it was possible to investigate further. They both correctly assumed that the murderer would have criminally active relatives, so they checked the database again, not to find a direct hit, but a close relative. They compiled a near complete DNA profile of Kappen from his spouse and relatives, but Williams' work is in some ways even more remarkable. His starting point was just one allele. He eventually found a close relative of the killer of Lynette White—his nephew—and Gafoor had not occurred previously as a suspect to suggest the coincidence that interested investigators in the Llandarcy crimes.

They had proved that familial DNA was now an important weapon in the fight against crime. It was also a useful tool in the struggle against miscarriages of justices. The real murderer of Lynette White was identified because the DNA data of a male member of his close family was on the database. Police forces throughout Britain know of this and it will be used in unsolved cases and possibly unresolved ones too, but what about those protesting innocence? It is very unlikely that this is the only miscarriage of justice that could be resolved with the conviction of the real perpetrator if the database was investigated in this manner, but surprisingly neither those protesting their innocence nor their legal representatives are demanding access to the database for that purpose. Why not?

CHAPTER 8

THE ARREST AND AFTERMATH

Unmasked

J EFFREY GAFOOR HAD KEPT HIS dark secret for 15 years. He had committed one of the most sadistic murders of its type in Welsh history in the early hours of Valentine's Day 1988 — a frenzied and vicious attack on a defenceless young woman that had sexual overtones to it. He slit her throat twice and continued to stab her more than 50 times. Not even her probable death satisfied his blood lust. Some of the injuries were inflicted on her as she was dying or even dead. The level of brutality was far beyond what was required to control or even kill Lynette.

Gafoor was an evil, sadistic killer, who slipped out of 7 James Street unnoticed and went home to get on with his life. He had several opportunities to come forward and take his punishment, but chose to enjoy his life at the expense of others. Gafoor did nothing to prevent what he alone knew for certain was a miscarriage of justice in the making when the Cardiff Five were arrested and charged with Lynette's murder. He stood idly by as they were forced to stand trial for his crime. He let three of them be convicted for Lynette's murder and still he said and did nothing. He let John and Ronnie Actie live with the stigma, the pointing of fingers and what he knew was an unjustified whispering campaign against them. He let their lives be ruined while he enjoyed his. He let the family life of the Cardiff Five be ripped apart. He stood idly by as three of them were forced to change into different people just to survive wrongful imprisonment for a bestial crime — one that could have resulted in them being maimed, disfigured or worse in prison.

Gafoor gave himself a chance of a life that he did not deserve without a second thought for the lives that he had ruined. Lynette's family had to cope not only with the terrible loss of their loved one in appalling circumstances, but also the guilt of having been wrong about the Cardiff Five. They had hated them but on an entirely false basis. Lynette's dad, the late Terry White, could easily have ended his days in prison having shot dead an innocent man. He believed that the Cardiff Five were guilty—the original investigators had convinced him. He never accepted John Actie's acquittal and confronted him with a gun. Had he opened fire he would have murdered an innocent man and ended his days in prison for it, while Gafoor continued to enjoy his ill-gotten freedom. Gafoor cared not a whit for any of the victims that his brutal actions had created. They have never recovered and probably never will. It is already too late for Ronnie Actie and Yusef Abdullahi—both died aged just 49, having seen Gafoor unmasked, but both were shamefully denied assistance to help rebuild their lives—and that might have prolonged their lives.

Gafoor thought that he could simply shut out his crime and live out the rest of his life without facing the consequences, but he had miscalculated. Kevin O'Neill and Brent Parry had no intention of allowing Lynette's murder to remain unresolved and unknown to him Paul Williams was closing in. The killer's days of undeserved freedom were running out. Almost two-and-a-half years after Tony Rogers announced that the murder was being reopened, Operation Mistral was about to make history. Williams had the satisfaction of being one of the officers to request a mouth swab from Gafoor for DNA-testing. Gafoor's comments established that he was the prime suspect—the boy's father had already been eliminated. Astonishingly he voluntarily gave a swab and secret surveillance was approved on Gafoor. It proved to be a wise decision, as Gafoor knew that his time was up. The next knock on his door would be to arrest him. He knew that he faced life imprisonment, but ever the coward he was determined to cheat justice if he could. He spent the evening of February 28th 2003 buying quantities of paracetamol from various shops. He then went home and prepared to die by overdosing on the drug.

Too Easy

Gafoor hoped that he would be able to take the easy way out. He took more than 60 tablets and waited to die, but that would have been too easy. Gafoor deserved to live and stand trial—Lynette's family, the Cardiff Five and their families had waited too long for him to be allowed to cheat justice so easily.

The surveillance meant that police suspected that he was trying to take his life and they had no intention of allowing him to continue to take the easy way out. At 9.30 in the evening they smashed-in his door and an ambulance arrived to take him to hospital. He was arrested and denied taking anything. He had clearly attempted suicide, realising that his past was about to catch up with him. Police acted swiftly to save his life and make him take responsibility for his sadistic crime after 15 years of cheating justice. He began to convulse and then made an unsolicited comment in the ambulance: "Just for the record, I did kill Lynette White," he said. "I have been waiting for 15 years for this. Whatever happens to me, I deserve."

Ambulance staff and police heard the comment. It was noted down. Gafoor didn't die. His life was saved in hospital as he was given the antidote to the paracetamol poisoning that he was suffering from. On March 1st he had recovered sufficiently to talk to police in hospital. "I would rather not die," he told police. "I would rather face the music, but I was looking forward to death to find out if God exists or the devil."

Gafoor had made admissions in the ambulance and in hospital, but they were not under the protections of formal interviews. Consequently, they could have been contested at his trial and ruled inadmissible because he did not have the protection of a solicitor and tape-recording, although the admissions were unsolicited and witnessed by independent people, such as the ambulance staff who helped to save his life.

If Gafoor decided to contest what the police alleged through his lawyers, the trial judge would have to decide on the admissibility of these admissions, but this was not "verballing" — the infamous practice of claiming that suspects had made incriminating remarks in the cells or in cars on the way to police stations after they had not confessed in interviews. This was totally different because there were independent witnesses who verified what police claimed that Gafoor had said and that nobody prompted him to do so. Verbals don't have independent corroboration, but this did. Gafoor intended the admissions in the ambulance to be his dying confession, but he hadn't reckoned on the determination of police and medical staff to save his life. The comments in the hospital were not unequivocal admissions, but suggested that he had something to answer for. He would soon have the opportunity to take responsibility for his crime under caution, but Gafoor had evaded justice for 15 years and wasn't ready to give up just yet. He was released into police custody on March 4th. He said, "I've got nothing to say."

Arrest and Aftermath

Gafoor spent the next week recovering in hospital. On March 7th he was fit enough to be interviewed. He was cautioned and subsequently charged. He was represented by Bernard de Maid, who had represented Yusef Abdullahi at his trials and appeal. That could have become a conflict of interest, but only if Gafoor tried to defend himself by claiming that he was innocent because the Cardiff Five were guilty. If that had been his intention, de Maid would have had to withdraw, but there was no indication of what his defence would be then.

Gafoor had the opportunity to repeat his "death-bed confession" during the formal police interviews. He declined to do so. He gave no comment interviews, effectively telling police to prove his guilt. This was his right, but adverse inferences — supporting evidence against him — could be drawn from his silence. Gafoor was remanded to prison and left to contemplate his options.

The stakeholders were informed of developments rapidly and the CPS became involved. They charged Gafoor with Lynette's murder and set about preparing the case against him. Without a confession it could have been a harder task, but O'Neill and his team, especially Parry and Williams, had done their job well. They had conducted a thorough investigation for two-and-a-half years and they had the advantage of being scrutinised at every stage. The Lay Advisory Group had seen every twist and turn of the investigation. It had been an open investigation in its own way and would therefore be difficult to discredit.

They had admissions from Gafoor, but not while under caution. They knew that he could choose to contest their admissibility and that they would have to defend them if he went down that route. However, their case against Gafoor did not depend on anything Gafoor had to say. They had circumstantial evidence. When asked for a mouth swab, Gafoor immediately tried to establish an excuse for the discovery of his DNA in the flat, but it was an explanation that did not stand up to scrutiny. He said that he was a client and asked if it was from semen. He was a client, but the DNA did not come from semen. His excuse could not explain the numerous traces of his blood that had been found in the flat and on the way out. Operation Mistral had been a great success as O'Neill and his team meticulously investigated the case and compiled a compelling case against Gafoor based on DNA.

The case against Gafoor stood or fell on the scientific evidence. They had obtained full DNA profiles from the blood on Lynette's jeans: her left sock, the inside of the communal door to 7 James Street, the inside of the door of Flat 1, 7 James Street, the cardboard box, the piece of cellophane, the skirting board and on the walls in the living room and hallway. The DNA profiles obtained from all of these items came from blood that had been deposited by one man and that man was directly involved in the murder. The DNA profiles obtained from each of those items matched that of Gafoor. The evidence clearly established that his blood could not have been planted at the crime scene and also that South Wales Police had no opportunity to do so even if they had the inclination.

Gafoor was a loner. He was a punter of Lynette's but nobody had heard of him before. Despite his use of prostitutes his name had not been offered to police in 1988 by any of the women who worked the Cardiff beats. He had not come to the attention of the police before Lynette's murder and he only had one conviction afterwards. The original investigators did not know of him at all and until Williams discovered that the murderer was a man from Gafoor's family, nor had O'Neill and his team.

How could they plant evidence to implicate a man they didn't even know existed? It was obvious that Gafoor had serious problems. How could he explain the scientific findings? Scene of crime photographs proved that the various blood-stains had indeed been shed and noted back in 1988. Not all of them were suitable for conventional blood grouping tests, nor the early DNA-testing systems. All items were packaged, sealed and stored for over a decade. They were recovered by officers looking to locate possible samples for DNA-testing. Some of these items matched the DNA profile of the killer and they also recovered sources of DNA from beneath paintwork. This would be the crux of the case against Gafoor and he knew that he would have serious problems explaining it away. He made appearances in court to verify who he was and received disclosure of the case against him. It was compelling. He had almost four months to decide what to do. He had challenged police to prove their case against him during his interviews. His first major appearance was set for July 4th 2003 and history was about to be made.

CHAPTER 9

GUILTY — HISTORY IS MADE

Remand

GAFOOR HAD A LOT TO think about. He had chosen to make the police prove their case by giving no comment interviews. However, if a judge ruled that the comments that he made in the ambulance were admissible they could be used against him. He had been arrested and cautioned when he made them, but he was suffering from paracetamol poisoning and they were made without a solicitor being present or the protection of tape-recording. He was hardly fit for interview, but these comments were unsolicited and they had been witnessed by ambulance staff who could verify what was said and that they were made voluntarily. Consequently, these admissions did not depend on the police who heard them to verify that they had been made by Gafoor and that they had not been solicited in any way. There were also the admissions that were made in the hospital after Gafoor recovered from the paracetamol poisoning. They were made to police officers and may have been easier for Gafoor to contest. If those comments were responses to questions by police officers, then it could have been a big problem that he didn't have a solicitor present at a time that he was clearly suspected of Lynette's murder. Those comments could have been ruled inadmissible, because the conversation could easily have been termed an "off the record" interview that breached the requirements of the Police and Criminal Evidence Act 1984. But Gafoor had far more serious problems than those admissions.

While he was in prison on remand the CPS complied with disclosure obligations. Bernard de Maid saw that the police had a strong case against him and instructed John Charles Rees QC to represent him at the first important hearing. Rees had also been involved in the trials of the Cardiff Five. He had been junior counsel for John Actie at the first trial — led by the then leader of the Wales and Chester Circuit, John Rogers QC (later to become

His Honour Judge Rogers, the senior judge of North Wales, who retired from the bench in 2010) — and had represented Actie himself at the second trial. If Gafoor tried to offer the defence that he was innocent because John Actie was guilty, then Rees would have had to withdraw due to a conflict of interest. Neither de Maid nor Rees had to withdraw from Gafoor's defence as there was no suggestion that either of their previous clients Yusef Abdullahi or John Actie were guilty. Gafoor's defence made no suggestion that any of the Cardiff Five were guilty. Abdullahi in particular wasn't happy that his old solicitor would represent the man accused of the crime that he had been wrongfully accused of previously. Nevertheless, after consulting colleagues, they were assured that there was no conflict of interest, so both de Maid and Rees set to work trying to prepare a defence for Gafoor. They received the crux of the prosecution case — the scientific evidence. How could this be explained away? It was damning. Gafoor could try to question the integrity of the investigation, or he could try to impugn the accuracy of the scientific evidence or both, or he could ditch his legal team and try to blame the original defendants. The alternative was to break the habit of a lifetime and take responsibility for his crimes.

Guilty

Gafoor's most important court appearance occurred on July 4th 2003 at Cardiff Crown Court. Members of Lynette's family were there and so were Tony Paris and his family. Yusef Abdullahi waited outside, not wanting to go inside the court. Michael O'Brien was there as well. He wanted to see Gafoor in the flesh — the first truly guilty murderer in Britain to have been caught after a miscarriage of justice. I was there too — it was the culmination, or so I naïvely thought then, of 12 years work on the case. Tony Paris was beaming from ear to ear. "They got him," he said.

The judge was Mr Justice (Sir John) Royce and the CPS had instructed Patrick Harrington QC. Gafoor was due to plead for the first time. There had been no indication what his plea would be. He confirmed his identity and then pleaded guilty. It was over. A major miscarriage of justice had been resolved in Britain for the first time by the conviction of the real murderer.

Operation Mistral had made history and my previous book had achieved its first major purpose within five years. Royce decided that the evidence should be heard anyway, beginning with the prosecution case, but who was Gafoor and how did he evade capture for so long?

Gafoor kept his own counsel. He was of mixed race — his father Indian and his mother Welsh. She died while he was young, so the young Gafoor lived with his father in the Roath district of Cardiff. He later lived rough before moving around several flats in Cardiff. He came to prefer to avoid what he viewed as unnecessary human contact. Despite living close to a then landlord, Gafoor never popped round to give him the rent or even to put it under his door. He would drive to the nearest post-box and post it. This was typical of him. He went out of his way to avoid human contact. He briefly worked in Germany while the Cardiff Three were in prison and acquired a reputation of being vehemently, but not violently opposed to pornography, but Gafoor's activities in Germany were not fully investigated. It is therefore unclear if he committed any crimes there. He didn't socialise in Germany either. Despite travelling with his brother, Gafoor chose to keep himself to himself.

He adopted the same approach in Britain. In 1992 he viciously attacked a colleague at work with a brick. He was ordered to do community service. It was his only other known crime. Two years before his arrest for Lynette's murder he bought a house in Llanharan — a village near Bridgend. It had been a family house previously. Gafoor liked it there, but made no effort to socialise or get to know his neighbours. He continued to stay aloof from other people, but collected bric-a-brac and antiques. The villagers were hurt to discover that they had a murderer living in their midst. Gafoor did not entertain visitors and had few if any friends. He didn't go out socially and tended to just watch television and go to work. It seemed as if the killer was shocked by his crime and determined never to put himself in a position where that could happen again. He became a complete loner.

Harrington's Case

Patrick Harrington QC told the court how Operation Mistral had tracked Gafoor down. He began by outlining the history of the case, starting with Lynette's murder. Harrington went through the Hacking Review resulting in the case being re-opened. He took his time over Operation Mistral and the scientific investigations, going into detail of how the scientists had obtained DNA profiles from the samples, especially the ones that were sealed in by paint. This involved specific protocols to ensure that the blood was extracted without damaging the DNA and to test the samples once extracted. Full profiles were obtained from several samples that had all been deposited in Flat 1, 7 James Street by Gafoor.

Harrington detailed Gafoor's history. "He was intelligent—a reader," said the QC. "He recognised the onward march of forensic science and the capture of criminals as a result of DNA techniques." Gafoor feared that police would eventually catch up with him because of advances in forensic science. He kept up to date with developments both in DNA techniques and the case. He had no need of trophies, or cuttings from the case. It was not something that he wanted to be reminded of. He preferred to try to block it out completely—well almost.

The prosecution's case was strong. Gafoor recognised that and pleaded guilty because he realised that after demanding that the police prove him guilty, they had in effect done so. Forensic science had trapped him. He listened impassively as Harrington told the court how police tracked him down after forensic science had given them the lead they required. He singled out detective constable Williams for praise, which was echoed by the judge. Williams deserved the praise.

Gafoor Responds

The court and public gallery were waiting, anticipating hearing Gafoor account for his actions. There were several questions that needed answers by cross-examination if necessary. The most important was why he had killed Lynette, especially in such a sadistic fashion?

"If I ever meet him I'd like to ask him why he did that to Lynette," Stephen Miller said. He never met Gafoor and never got a satisfactory answer to his question — the least that Gafoor could do after the ordeal he inflicted on the Cardiff Five by doing nothing when he alone knew that they were paying for his crime. He had the opportunity to explain why he had allowed innocent men and their families to suffer for his crimes.

Ever the coward Gafoor declined to speak himself. He left it to Rees to explain the unconscionable actions that had brought him to court. Rees began by saying what a good thing it was that capital punishment had been abolished. He told the court that Gafoor was a recluse, before trying to explain his actions after the murder. "He blanked his memory, so he could live with himself," Rees said. "He cut himself off. He told police that it was a relief that he was caught."

So far this was coming across as a pathetic attempt at self-justification. Where was the remorse? Where was the acknowledgement of what Gafoor had done to all of his victims? After 15 years he had the opportunity to give the Cardiff Five, their families and Lynette's too, the small comfort of at least understanding why they had suffered. Why did he kill Lynette? Gafoor said nothing. Again he answered through Rees. "This was not a premeditated or sexual killing," said Rees.

Nonsense in my view; it may not have been premeditated, but it certainly had sexual overtones to it. He went out looking for a prostitute and viciously attacked her. It may not have been a classic sex offence, but it was a sexual killing. He repeatedly stabbed her breasts. Her left breast was almost cut off. How was this not a sexual crime? But even worse was to follow — the closest to an explanation of his crime that Gafoor ever gave.

Gafoor put an outrageously low value on Lynette's life and that occurred because of his utterly hypocritical views on prostitution. If he opposed prostitution so much and thought he had the right to look down on them there was a simple solution — don't use their services. Sadly that never occurred to him. He chose to use Lynette. He initiated the transaction precisely because he wanted to have sex with a prostitute. It was his choice to initiate that transaction. All she did was agree to it, but he took the power of life and death over her. Miller, his co-defendants, Lynette's family and society have a right to know why. According to him Lynette's life was not worth

£30. "He went to the docks to seek the services of a prostitute," said Rees. "He met Lynette White and went back to her flat, where he paid her £30, but he changed his mind and asked for his money back. He was carrying a knife because he had been robbed three months before in Butetown. In the course of the argument he took the knife out and threatened her with it. She grabbed the knife and there was a struggle, during which she was stabbed. He doesn't know why what followed, followed. There was shame, panic and there was a frenzied attack with a knife."

What? That is his explanation for the most vicious and sadistic murder of its type in Welsh history at that time. He expects people to believe it occurred because he wanted a refund of £30 after changing his mind on using the services of a prostitute. Rees went on to say that the murder was an extraordinary and terrible event in Gafoor's life and that otherwise Gafoor had lived a normal life. Words fail. Gafoor had the opportunity to take full responsibility for his crime and tell Lynette's family why he had killed her. He could also have given the Cardiff Five the satisfaction of knowing why he committed the crime that ruined their lives. Instead, he made a pathetic and self-serving plea for understanding without honesty. Nobody could seriously believe that a dispute over £30 could lead to such violence, especially in a man with no previous convictions. The very least Gafoor could do was tell the truth. Why did he really kill Lynette? The attack had obvious sexual overtones to it, which suggests that he took pleasure from inflicting such pain on her. Even after her death was inevitable he continued inflicting further pain on her. Why was it such a brutal and sadistic attack? Lynette's family and the Cardiff Five and their families and society deserve to know the truth and only he can give them that. He shouldn't have the luxury of blocking it out, as only he can give all of his victims closure by understanding the circumstances that led to their suffering. He will be released eventually, but that should not happen until he fully explains his crime. How else can it be decided whether it is safe to release him?

To his credit Harrington was not about to let Gafoor off the hook so lightly. "After the killing [Gafoor's] life appears to have continued on an even keel," he said. "Only he knew the secret of what he had done and that secret he still keeps. Police interviewed him extensively, but he told them that he had nothing to say — he has answered no questions about the murder."

Gafoor does not deserve to get off so easily. He has made no effort to take responsibility when it mattered and still hasn't. Even now, more than eight years through his sentence he has not had the common decency to explain what happened and why. Gafoor was the only person who had the power to prevent a miscarriage of justice and give Lynette's family justice. He chose to savour his freedom for the next 15 years instead while the lives of all of his victims were ruined. Once he was brought to justice, he offered pathetic self-serving lies rather than the full and frank explanation his victims had waited so long to hear. The cowardly murderer did not even have courage to apologise in person. After he was brought to justice Gafoor apologised to Lynette's family and the Cardiff Three, but did so through Rees. Too little, too late. The bare minimum they all deserved was an apology in his own words from his own mouth and the truth, but Gafoor denied them even that small courtesy.

The Aftermath

Mr Justice Royce sentenced Jeffrey Gafoor to life imprisonment. "You ended a young life in the most terrible way and for 15 years you kept your guilty secret and evaded justice, even as others faced trial for the murder you knew you committed," Royce told the now convicted killer. He also said that he thought the fact that he had allowed five innocent men to spend a total of 16 years in prison for his crime was the most serious aggravating circumstance. Gafoor's QC joined calls for a public inquiry into the original case and South Wales Police anticipated these calls, but they were determined to put their own house in order themselves. Tony Paris expressed delight that Gafoor had been caught, rather euphemistically describing him as "a horrible person". He hoped that Gafoor would spend the rest of his life in prison. He deserves it.

Outside the court the head of South Wales Police CID, DCS Wynne Phillips, scored what to my mind was a spectacular own goal. He held an impromptu press conference on the steps of the court. Phillips told the assembled journalists that it was a great day for justice and that it was all about justice for Lynette. But there were other victims of that case. What about justice for them? Paris had heard as much as he could tolerate. He demanded an apology. He should have received it immediately, but Phillips tried to fob him off. "Clearly, there is some work to do now in terms of looking back at the original trial," said Phillips. "The inquiry into the trial, being carried out in conjunction with the Crown Prosecution Service is ongoing and for that reason it would be inappropriate to discuss the matter any further."

Nonsense; Paris wanted an apology—he was surely due that as an absolute minimum. So the above was a surprising response from DCS Phillips as it seemed obvious that the force would have to apologise at the highest level before long. How difficult was it to say that the force apologises unreservedly to the Cardiff Five and their families for the force's role in their wrongful convictions or accusations? Instead Phillips gave the media a story that actually took the gloss off their triumph.

On Monday July 7th Sir Anthony Burden, the chief constable, apologised in writing to each of the Cardiff Five and Lynette's family. They also began what is known as Phase Three—Operation Rubicon—led by detective chief superintendent Chris Coutts. Its terms of reference were to investigate any allegations of criminal conduct by anyone in the original inquiry. Meanwhile, I met Kevin O'Neill, Brent Parry and Paul Williams. They were understandably pleased with the outcome, but O'Neill was fiercely critical of the original investigation.[1]

Tony Rogers could also bask in the success. He had taken the difficult decision not to disclose material despite his promises, because he believed there was a chance of finding the real killer. He was vindicated on July 4th 2003 by a team of exceptionally good police officers and forensic scientists who had conducted a model investigation and made history, largely due to their skills. They deserved to celebrate a fantastic result and receive the credit that their painstaking investigation had earned. They shut up many critics that day. Their methods were flawless and their integrity beyond question.

---

1. I had been promised interviews with Parry, O'Neill and Williams, which were needed for this book. After the investigation into what went wrong began three days later, the police decided that those interviews would have to wait until the process was over. That happened in December 2011. I renewed the request and was told that it would not happen until after the new investigation into the collapse of the trial of eight police officers and two witnesses had ended: see generally *Chapter 13*. The book had previously been delayed due to the trial itself and I did not wish to delay it any further, so decided to go ahead without the interviews.

They deserve to be appreciated for a superb job, but that was also the greatest disaster for their force, as it proved beyond doubt that the Cardiff Five were innocent and that they had been the victims of a gross miscarriage of justice. They were the first in Britain to be vindicated in the DNA age by the conviction of the real killer and their vindication opened the door for others. However, there were other issues that needed answers being given to them too.

What made Gafoor tick? Understanding that may help to prevent other Gafoors, his behaviour being impossible to predict. Are there other killers like Gafoor out there? If so, how can they be detected quickly and efficiently?

CHAPTER 10

CHARACTERISTICS OF A KILLER

Error of Judgement

OFFENDER PROFILING, POPULARISED BY TELEVISION programmes like "Cracker" and "NCIS" was in its infancy 20 years ago, at least in Britain, but the murder of Lynette White was to prove as important a case for it as that of Rachel Nickell. The sometimes controversial profiler Paul Britton was at the height of his fame when he helped devise a strategy to investigate the murder of the young model. On July 15th 1992, Nickell was stabbed repeatedly in broad daylight on Wimbledon Common in front of her two-year-old son, Alex. It was an appalling crime that had to be solved quickly, but the police got it badly wrong. Their enquiries became fixed on a man who seemed to fit the bill, but this person, Colin Stagg, was innocent. The real killer was an extremely dangerous individual who would kill again, Robert Napper.

Stagg used to frequent Wimbledon Common and was said to have an interest in the occult. The whole case against him was a result of an attempt to take offender profiling beyond its limits. Britton compiled a profile that investigators came to believe fitted Stagg and he helped to devise an investigative strategy that involved an undercover policewoman, referred to as Lizzie James, posing as a potential girlfriend to obtain a confession — a honey-trap that would not have been out of place at the height of Cold War espionage.

Paul Britton now explains that it was not his own strategy, but that of the police, although this interpretation has been denied by detective inspector Keith Pedder, the head of the Rachel Nickell murder investigation. Whatever the true situation, letters were used to lure Stagg into a police trap. At Stagg's subsequent trial in 1994, Mr Justice (Sir Harry) Ognall threw out Stagg's alleged admissions and the CPS was forced to offer no evidence, as it had nothing else with which to establish its case.

Stagg endured an unjustified whispering campaign that was finally silenced in December 2008 when Napper—a schizophrenic who was responsible for a five year reign of terror—was tied to Nickell's murder. Napper was the Green Chain Rapist—the person allegedly responsible for a series of 86 offences (but of which few have been proved: see later in this chapter), including the rape of a woman who was pushing a pram. Those crimes had been linked to Nickell's murder before and after Stagg's arrest, but the police fixation on Stagg had terrible consequences for him. DNA would eventually prove that Napper was indeed her killer, but years earlier there had been plenty of reason to suspect him. It was bad enough that offender profiling had led the police to pursue the innocent Stagg, but this paled into insignificance compared to Napper taking advantage of the lack of interest in him to commit further appalling crimes. Police attention on the Green Chain Rapes had forced Napper out of his comfort zone in search of victims. It was Nickell's misfortune to encounter him on Wimbledon Common.

Incredibly, the police ignored strong evidence that Napper was the real killer. Napper's mother, Pauline Lasham had tipped them off that he had confessed to her that he had raped a woman on Plumstead Common in South-East London in November 1989, but they ignored this because they failed to find a crime that matched that admission—the victim lived in a house that backed onto Plumstead Common. It was a missed opportunity that could have saved Nickell's life, spared Stagg his ordeal, saved two more lives and prevented other rapes too.

With Stagg in prison on remand awaiting trial for "Napper's crime", Napper's blood lust resurfaced. He seized his opportunity in November 1993, breaking into Samantha Bissett's flat in Plumstead while her boyfriend was out, sexually assaulting her and stabbing her eight times. Her four-year-old daughter Jazmine was smothered and sexually assaulted as well. These were the crimes that resulted in Napper being detained indefinitely in Broadmoor Special Hospital, but he had left a trail of evidence which pointed to him having committed the Green Chain crimes but that had been missed.

Napper's reign of terror could have been halted before lives were lost. Just two months before Nickell was murdered, a Green Chain Rape victim came frighteningly close to becoming Napper's first murder victim. She begged for her life and was spared. The e-fit bore a striking resemblance to him, but two failed attempts to obtain samples from him for DNA-testing resulted in that investigation stalling.

By mid-1992 Napper had begun to leave his South-East London stomping ground in search of other victims. Stagg was seen walking his dog on Wimbledon Common on July 15th 1992. Napper was also there and would commit his first murder. Police, focussed on Stagg, but the evidence against him was wafer thin, so Lizzie James was used to try to obtain a confession. Stagg tried to please her, but he couldn't give her the confession she wanted because he had not committed the offence. He might not have conformed to society's demands, but he did not kill Rachel Nickell and targeting him was inappropriate. There was no solid (or indeed any other) evidence for this, he was just an "unconventional" individual.

Lizzie James subsequently left the police, claiming that she had suffered stress from the case and was awarded £125,000 compensation in 2001. Stagg eventually received over £700,000 compensation and the botched inquiry cost £3 million. It remains a fiasco for offender profiling and for the CJS (with the notable exception of the part played by Mr Justice Ognall who ruled that the honey-trap evidence was inadmissible). Nonetheless it has to be emphasised that a charge brought by the British Psychological Society against Britton was dismissed in 2002.

Napper has only admitted to six crimes — three murders and three rapes. He is suspected of many more, especially the Green Chain Rapes, but he is going nowhere. He is being detained indefinitely at Broadmoor and it is likely that he will never be considered safe to release. He admitted the manslaughter of Samantha and Jazmine Bissett and later that of Rachel Nickell as well on the basis of diminished responsibility. Bissett's parents and partner are convinced that Napper should never have been free at the relevant time, because they considered that he was the real killer of Nickell — and they were right. Napper refuses to talk to the police about other crimes unless they first produce scientific evidence linking him to them.

It was DNA evidence that eventually persuaded Robert Napper to admit to killing Rachel Nickell, 16 years later. Mr Justice Ognall described the attempt to entrap Stagg as, "deceptive conduct of the grossest kind". Whatever Britton's role in that case or his explanations, it has been questioned even by fellow practitioners of offender profiling as well as for breaking guidelines on confidentiality, but the Lynette White Inquiry was another important failure for the "science"of offender profiling, even if it has not received the attention it deserves.

Professor Canter's Offender Profile of Lynette White's Killer

By May 1988 it was clear that the Lynette White Inquiry was not going to be resolved quickly. The police had already traced and eliminated many people, but the inquiry was in need of a fresh impetus. The police turned to Professor David Canter— a leading expert and "the father of offender profiling" in Britain—to try to generate new lines of inquiry. Canter produced a psychological profile offering likely character traits of the killer. He analysed crime scene reports and other material to try to establish a potential motive for the murder and the psychological traits of the killer. He also tried to establish a relationship between Lynette and her killer. In his book *Criminal Shadows*, he says that this profile led police to Stephen Miller and the rest of the Cardiff Five).[1]

The unused condom on the bed and use of the flat for prostitution suggested that the killer was a punter, but Lynette White was fully clothed apart from a shoe and her jacket, which was half-on-half-off. According to Canter that suggested someone other than a client. Why? It was equally consistent with the attack occurring before she had undressed and that it had been committed by a client who had changed his mind—which is exactly what Gafoor later claimed had happened. The eminent forensic pathologist Professor Bernard Knight said that Lynette hadn't been interfered with sexually, but the attack had sexual overtones and was consistent with an attack by a client.

Canter's assessment of the relationship between Lynette and her killer was that she probably went to the flat with a client. He believed that the killer was prone to sudden violent attacks and was likely to be known to the police either from his sudden violence or lack of control. The killer was likely to be familiar with the area from using prostitutes or knew Lynette's

---

1. See *Criminal Shadows: Inside the Mind of the Serial Killer* (1995), David Canter, London: Harper Collins. This was written before Jeffrey Gafoor was identified as the true killer and it would naturally have been a strange claim to have made afterwards.

habits. Canter thought that the aspermic semen was significant and that the attack was disorganized and unplanned—a very sudden attack against an individual that had aroused feelings of anger in the murderer, or represented something that angered him, or made him lose control. According to Canter, the attacker was likely to have had poor mental abilities and a history of impulsive behaviour, to have been unable to cope with social relationships and to have had an intermittent and unskilled employment history.

He thought that the attack indicated a drug or alcohol-induced state and expressed the opinion that the killer had attempted to hide Lynette's identity by removing her head and hands, but had abandoned the attempt. He found this aspect bizarre and thought that it indicated a mentally disturbed killer who burst out into uncontrollable rages. He believed that the killer had a history of violent attacks and the failure to complete the attempt to hide her identity suggested remorse. He thought that her killer was known to her and that he was a previous client angered by her earlier absence and was overcome with anger as she began to undress.

Canter also suggested that the killer was likely to have had severe mental disturbance that had resulted in imprisonment or hospitalisation and he was likely to have come from a broken home with a history of violence in it. Nevertheless, he believed that the murderer would confess if confronted forcefully and might have already admitted the offence to someone, although the unsocial characteristics of the killer might deprive him of contact with others to confess to. He also suggested that the existence of a highly controlling client or linking the murder to other similar crimes could affect the results and that witnesses could be withholding information, especially if Lynette had screamed. He suggested that the killer would not be trusted socially, but would have a base near the scene of the crime and would be in his early twenties, but that this was the thing he was most likely to be wrong about. Ironically, he got this part of his assessment spot on.

Another Interpretation

Professor Canter's profile may well have influenced the course of the police investigation but it did not lead the police to the true killer Jeffrey Gafoor.

117

It was used by detective inspector Graham Mouncher to support his request that a man who became the prime suspect should be put under surveillance, but that man was subsequently eliminated in November 1988. While that suspect fitted many of the characteristics identified by Canter, he was later proved to be innocent.

With hindsight, a review of the likely character traits of the killer identified by Canter bears no real resemblance to Gafoor, to Stephen Miller or any of the rest of the Cardiff Five. This exposes once again the limitations of offender profiling the standards of the time and the fact that it has since become far more obvious that it only works if it is fully integrated with other investigative tools (see my further comments on this aspect of profiling in *Chapter 11*).

The fact that the murderer was likely to have been a client of Lynette White's was hardly a revelation — it had been a fundamental line of inquiry from the start of the investigation. Also, for example, the state of her clothing was of limited relevance, as it depended on when the murderer decided to kill and why; it could still have been a client (and that turned out to be true). The assumption that the murderer would be known to the police for loss of control or sudden violent outbursts also turned out to be wrong. There is no evidence that Gafoor, the killer, had a base in Butetown — he lived in Cardiff, but was not known by prostitutes in the area. He claimed that he had been robbed by one in Butetown months earlier — the justification for him carrying a knife (but there is no independent evidence anyway that Gafoor's claim about being robbed was true).

The aspermic semen was insignificant. It remained unidentified and was not consistent with the state of Lynette's clothing. It has never been tied to the murderer and as such cannot be considered important. Canter's assumption that the murder was committed in an alcohol or drug-induced state was not supported by the forensic evidence, but he was correct in deducing that it was an unplanned and disorganized attack and that the victim had aroused feelings of anger that caused him to lose control (although some people might say that this was fairly obvious). The killer had just committed the most brutal murder of its type in Welsh history — clearly he was likely to be angry and have lost any normal kind of control. Canter's suggestion that the killer was angered by Lynette's earlier absence conflicts with the explanation offered by the killer himself. Gafoor claimed that he accompanied Lynette to the flat in 7 James Street to have sex with her, but after giving her £30 he changed his mind and demanded his money back. She refused and they argued. Gafoor then pulled a knife on her and stabbed her repeatedly. There is no evidence at all that Gafoor was angered by Lynette's earlier absence or even that he knew her previously.

The suggestion that the attacker would be likely to have poor mental abilities and a history of impulsive behaviour hardly fits Gafoor who is intelligent and read a lot. He was able to "blend in" because he seemed so ordinary. He certainly was not known for impulsive behaviour, let alone did he have a known history of it and he had no existing convictions for violence or any other offences. Gafoor was not known to the police and if he was prone to uncontrollable rages, the police had no inkling of that.

So what was there to support the explanation for the alleged attempt to remove Lynette's head and hands? The fact that the killer had been taken to the flat by Lynette for prostitution suggests that it was highly unlikely her identity would remain a secret for long. The killer knew that she was a prostitute and that this was her place of business. Why would the killer assume that the police would not suspect who she was?

As to the killer being likely to have had severe mental disturbance that had resulted in imprisonment or hospitalisation, Gafoor had not been hospitalised nor imprisoned. And as to the murderer being likely to have come from a broken home with a history of violence in it and that he would not be trusted socially, there is no evidence that Gafoor was not trusted socially nor that he came from a broken home. He lived with his father for a while out of necessity, but because his mother had died. The police are not aware of violence in the family home as he was growing up. Canter believed that the killer would have had a base near the scene of the crime. Gafoor grew up in Splott and Ely—districts on the other side of Cardiff. The police never found evidence that he was known among prostitutes in Butetown or anything that linked him generally to that area.

Canter suggested that the killer would be in his 20s, but that he could be wrong about that. He turned out to be quite close. Gafoor was just 22 at the time of the murder. He also believed that the murderer would have been unable to cope with social relationships and have had an intermittent and unskilled employment history. But does it not have to be asked whether it was too early to assign such characteristics to such a young killer? Gafoor subsequently chose to avoid unnecessary human contact, but that was largely due to his having murdered Lynette White, not a trait that is known to have existed before the murder took place. He cut himself off from his family five years after he murdered Lynette and went to Germany with one of his brothers in 1992. His reclusiveness appears to have manifested itself after he returned from Germany not before. He may not have had many friends, but he was not the outcast Canter appears to have thought him to be at the time of the murder and he never explained why the killer was likely to be so young, or how such a youthful person matched other characteristics of his profile.

While Gafoor was not confronted forcefully—he was interviewed in a different era and there was no need for that anyway—the Cardiff Five were interviewed in a forceful manner and it resulted in Stephen Miller being bullied and hectored until he confessed to a crime he knew he had not committed. The only admissions Gafoor made were after an overdose that he hoped would be fatal (see *Chapter 8*). As soon as he recovered, he made the police prove their case. Gafoor was not a highly controlling client. There is no evidence that he had any previous relationship with Lynette and despite thorough searches of the National DNA Database and other investigations, he has never been linked to any other unsolved crime.

Accountability

As previously indicated, offender profiling led police to investigate a particular suspect, a middle-aged paedophile who could be tied to both Lynette and to two of the alleged eyewitnesses. He had a similar combination of blood groups to the killer, a long history of offences against children and had been imprisoned. He was such an outcast in his community that three years before the murder of Lynette White a neighbour lost control and inflicted severe injuries some of which were of a similar type to those suffered by Lynette. She received a non-custodial sentence despite attacking him with a meat cleaver. This man had a proven gripe against women and used prostitutes, including Lynette White. The police came to suspect him themselves and it does seem that he was the person that fitted Canter's profile most accurately despite some differences. He was placed under surveillance after detective inspector Mouncher acknowledged that he fitted Canter's profile. The man was eliminated in November 1988.

Much of what I have described above seems to have done the discipline of offender profiling as it stood in the late 1980s few favours and the past still resonates. If offender profiling is to be a genuinely useful tool, there must be accountability and a system of accreditation to ensure quality control. Both the Rachel Nickell Inquiry and Lynette White Inquiry graphically demonstrate the need for such a system. Paul Britton has faced criticism for his role in the Colin Stagg case, even by Professor Canter, but some lessons have been learned. The National Crime and Operations Faculty (NCOF) runs a system that accredits such experts as described in the the next chapter.

CHAPTER 11

LESSONS — PROFILING GAFOOR

A Pitiless Coward

FOR 15 YEARS JEFFREY GAFOOR lived with his guilty secrets and avoided the consequences of his actions as best he could. Five innocent men and their families had their lives ruined while he stood by and watched. And Lynette's family too had their lives torn apart more than once. They had learned to cope by hating the Cardiff Five, but Gafoor alone knew for certain that their hatred was misplaced. Even after Terry White confronted John Actie with a gun, Gafoor did nothing. Actie could have been shot dead for a brutal murder that Gafoor knew he had not committed. Ever the coward, Gafoor stayed silent, hoping it would go away even if that cost another innocent person their life. Gafoor had neither pity nor remorse for his actions then, so can his apology and supposed remorse be believed now?

"I am sure that he would have been totally distraught and upset by what he had done which he would have carried with him for 15 years", Professor Canter told Tony Barratt of the *Liverpool Echo*,[1] but according to my interpretation Gafoor's actions seem to tell a different story. This was a man who had ample opportunity to come forward in 15 years and did nothing while five men he knew to be innocent beyond any doubt lost a total of 16 years of their lives. If Professor Canter acknowledges this, it is not so far as I can discern reflected in Barratt's article, which fails to even mention the Cardiff Five, let alone their ordeal, or the effect of what Gafoor did to them.

Where then is the evidence that Gafoor was "totally distraught" by what he had done? He had several opportunities to come forward and address his offending behaviour and the consequences of his crime. He had committed

---

1. See "The Man Whose Job it is to Get Inside the Mind of a Killer, Tony Barratt looks at the work of Liverpool's murder-solving professor", *Liverpool Echo*, August 19th 2003.

a murder that was then the most savage of its kind in Welsh history. If he was as distraught and upset by what he had done as he would like people to believe—about a crime that appeared totally out of character—he could have gone to the police and sought help. Why didn't he? It would have meant going to prison while showing that his remorse was genuine and prevented one of Britain's most notorious miscarriages of justice from happening, but Gafoor didn't surrender himself to the police. He wanted his freedom and showed by his inaction that he cared not a whit if innocent people paid for his crime with ruined lives.

The investigation into Lynette White's murder began in February 1988. Several lines of enquiry were pursued at length—taxi drivers, prostitutes and punters were traced, interviewed and eliminated, but not Gafoor. He chose to pay for Lynette's services on that night, knowing full well that she was a prostitute. It was the reason that he went with her after all. He had the opportunity to come forward then, but chose not to, preferring to stay silent and hope that it would just go away.

The police's fixation on Butetown and the Cardiff Five bought him years of undeserved liberty, but helped to establish Gafoor's true character. Even after his arrest Gafoor chose not to shed light on what had happened and why. He believed in DNA-testing, keeping up to date with developments in forensic science and developing strong views against pornography, but he cherished his freedom. In December 1988 the arrest and charging of the Cardiff Five was headline news, especially in South Wales. Gafoor knew for certain that innocent men were facing an unjust trial that would destroy their lives and those of their families and their community too. Perhaps he thought that they would be acquitted, but three of them were convicted; he still stayed silent. Unlike him they could not express remorse, looking for early release on parole as that included giving details of the crime that they did not have, and more importantly, because they had nothing to be remorseful over. They didn't know what had happened to Lynette beyond what they had been told by the police, but Gafoor knew chapter and verse and in time he would make his guilty knowledge benefit him too.

Instead, they endured two further years of wondering if they would get shanked (stabbed or slashed with an improvised weapon) in prison or per-haps have boiling water that had been laced with sugar, or even boiling oil, thrown in their faces. They had been convicted of a bestial crime. All it took was one prisoner who believed them to be guilty or wanted to make a name for himself and they could have been disfigured for life. Prisoners make the harshest judges as they have too much time on their hands and have heard too many false claims of innocence.

As the late Yusef Abdullahi explained, "If [other prisoners] thought we were guilty, we would have been dealt with severely, very severely." All it took was one prisoner to decide to punish them in such a manner and they would be maimed or worse. They faced that every day for Gafoor's crime and he callously left them at risk of it. Stephen Miller's plight was even worse. He couldn't explain his actions beyond saying that he had been bullied and was embarrassed about his vulnerabilities. Prisoners did not understand or believe that such things happened and Miller refused to discuss his problems with other prisoners. Even though some of them guessed, it did nothing to address the real danger that he was in. Either he was a guilty self-confessed murderer of a young woman in a particularly sadistic manner, or he had falsely implicated innocent men, including himself. Both explanations were extremely hazardous to his health. He was fortunate that he was not attacked or maimed. Gafoor put Miller's health and even his life at risk, because he knew for certain that Miller's confession was complete nonsense and that his retraction of it was true.

Gafoor did nothing — not even an anonymous tip off to a journalist that only the killer could have known. For somebody that was supposed to be totally distraught and upset by his crime, surely remorse included that. He could at least have tried to prevent a miscarriage of justice from ruining more lives. Instead, he chose to sacrifice the Cardiff Five for his own ends. Their lives became defined by what happened to them rather than who they were. Gafoor played a large part in that. Even though two of them were acquitted in 1990 after two years in prison on remand, fingers still pointed unjustly at John and Ronnie Actie and when the remaining members of the Cardiff Five were released in December 1992 it was already too late for them too. The system did not acknowledge their innocence, let alone apologise to them as they deserved. They were left to fend for themselves and suffer another eleven years of tongues wagging and fingers pointing at them. They were stuck in a time warp from which there seemed to be no escape.

They could not rebuild their lives, because too many people believed that they had got off on a technicality, but Gafoor knew for certain that only he and the CJS had got away with it. The Cardiff Five were all free by December 1992, but so was Gafoor and unlike him they could not put the murder of Lynette White behind them so easily. It dogged them then and still does. They had to endure the cruel tongues, usually too cowardly to say anything to their faces and a system that simply did not know what to do with them. Meanwhile, Gafoor could have spared them that, but chose to enjoy his life at their expense. It became clear that Gafoor had no intention of ever owning up to his crime unless forced to do so—that isn't unusual, but far from rewarding such people for their cowardly behaviour, the CJS should punish them and only reward those whose remorse is genuine.

When the police knocked on Gafoor's door for a sample for DNA-testing they already knew that a male relation of his nephew was the real murderer. Realising that refusal would cause suspicion, Gafoor tried again to evade the consequences by claiming that his DNA could have be in the flat in James Street because he had had sex with Lynette. That was a lie as Gafoor knew only too well. He had deposited blood at various locations in the flat and on Lynette and he knew very well that he did not have sex with her that night. Are these the actions of a man who is "totally distraught" and "upset" by what he did?

DNA was about to tie him to his crime, but ever the coward Gafoor tried one last time to escape the consequences by attempting suicide. When that failed he refused to take responsibility until confronted with overwhelming evidence of his guilt; finally there was nowhere to hide. That appears to be the real Jeffrey Gafoor. As Tony Paris said, "He is evil for what he did to us."

Failing to Take Responsibility

Gafoor was the only person who knew how and why Lynette died. He had the legal right to demand that the police prove their case, but why would he do that if he felt truly sorry for what he had done? He could have given Lynette's family the small crumb of comfort of knowing exactly why he killed her. He could also have acknowledged that the Cardiff Five were innocent and explained why they served time for his crime, but yet again he took the coward's way out by saying "no comment" during police interviews. Four months later he pleaded guilty, but he knew how to play the system that was tailor made to help him rather than the innocent victims of his crime. His barrister, John Charles Rees QC told the court that Gafoor carried a knife because he knew about the notoriety of Butetown and he had been robbed by a prostitute before. He accompanied Lynette to the flat and gave her £30. She began to undress. He changed his mind and demanded his money back, which she refused. At some point he pulled the knife on her and lost his temper during a struggle.

That was the only explanation that Gafoor has ever given of why he killed Lynette White and even that came through his QC.[2] People had waited 15 years for him to explain why he had murdered Lynette and also why he allowed others to suffer for his crime, but he supplied answers concerning neither. Does he really expect people to believe that he committed such a vicious murder over a paltry £30? And if he did, then robbery was a motive that ought to have been taken into account in deciding the minimum term that he should serve in prison before being eligible for parole. Nothing could justify any of his conduct, but Gafoor apologised to both the Cardiff Five and Lynette's family only through his counsel. Was this supposed to be remorse? He had let them sweat and have their lives ruined for 15 years and then apologised through his lawyer. He didn't even have the decency to do it in person.

Unpredictable

Gafoor had an opportunity to help the police, the CJS and society understand what turned a seemingly ordinary young man into a vicious killer. He holds the key to helping to identify similar killers, thereby giving the

---

2. Gafoor gave evidence at the trial of eight police officers and two witnesses in Swansea Crown Court in 2011. As I was due to be a witness in that trial, I could not attend as an observer. The court reports do not suggest that he detailed his full reasons for murdering Lynette White and allowing the Cardiff Five to suffer for his crime. He did, however, insist that he had murdered her on his own.

smallest token of peace to all of the victims of this tragic case, but he chose not to give such insight and still hasn't. If he expects society to accept that his remorse is genuine, then he should help us understand what made him tick. What had turned him from a largely law-abiding young man into a sadistic killer? Society needs answers and only he can give them. He was a brutal murderer—nothing could change that and nothing could roll back the years and undo the damage that he has done. Nevertheless, the very least that he could do was give the Cardiff Five the scant satisfaction of knowing why their lives had been ruined and that he had belatedly taken responsibility to try to prevent others following his path.

He was a particularly frightening type of killer, because his character traits were so difficult to predict. He was both ordinary and unique and that made him impossible to unmask in 1988. He had not come to the attention of South Wales Police before Lynette's murder and didn't stand out in any way. Most killers, especially ones who kill in such a brutal fashion, have a previous criminal history of violent offences, or insanity, but none of this applied to Gafoor. This type of criminal activity often involves cruelty to animals in childhood. There are other "classic" signs, many of which Professor Canter predicted would be found in Lynette's killer (see generally *Chapter 10*). Gafoor's lack of criminal activity allowed him to pass under the police radar. Even his use of prostitutes was unknown to police and the prostitutes that shared Lynette's beat. Police interviewed numerous prostitutes who worked in Cardiff during the original investigation, but Gafoor's name was never mentioned. He did not conform to the likely characteristics of Lynette's killer at all—that was why he was so hard to find.

His behaviour before the murder gave no clues that he was capable of such brutality and there were no tell-tale signs afterwards either. Nobody who knew him at that time or later suspected that he was the real murderer. He didn't develop a taste for killing, or even violence as a result of it. He resumed his nondescript life, coping with what he had done by blocking it out completely. Weeks turned into months and then years and Gafoor moved to more desirable accommodation near Bridgend. He seemed respectable, blending into his new community easily, despite appearing peculiar because he kept himself to himself—nobody suspected that they were harbouring a particularly sadistic killer in their midst. He had become more unusual than he had been previously, but there was no reason to suspect the terrible secret that he was hiding. His neighbours don't want to talk any more about the killer that penetrated their community. That's their choice, but Gafoor is a different matter. He possesses the knowledge and insight that could prevent other killers like him striking again. Surely his debt to society should include an explanation.

The murder of Lynette White was the first criminal offence that Gafoor was known to have committed, although he later admitted to illegally carrying a knife for protection as he claimed to have been robbed by a prostitute. Gafoor exhibited none of the expected psychological or psychiatric trauma that could help to explain such a vicious crime. His behaviour was completely unpredictable and challenges the conventional wisdoms of offender profiling. Nobody could have expected that this would be his first offence, or that, having committed such a crime, he would not strike again, despite not being hospitalised or imprisoned.

Gafoor remained at liberty for 15 years after his crime. For four years he carried his guilt without any obvious sign that anything was wrong, enjoying his stolen liberty—freedom he savoured at the expense of innocent men. The Cardiff Five were no angels, but compared to him they were saints and had a far greater moral sense than he did. Even after everything that was done to them, they wanted justice for Lynette and they even helped the police in the reopened inquiry. Gafoor did not. Instead, he gave himself a second chance that he did not deserve or earn.

Meanwhile, the Cardiff Five had no choice but to go through an ordeal that his behaviour had caused them. Months before the remaining three overturned their wrongful convictions—no thanks to Gafoor—the cowardly killer committed another violent crime. He attacked a colleague with half a brick, beating him almost senseless. He avoided imprisonment, even though his offence merited it—community service and a fine was all he got.

Gafoor had another eleven years of ill-deserved liberty to enjoy. Once again he retreated into his shell and existed beneath the police radar. He did nothing to bring himself to the attention of the police for the decade following the attack on his work colleague. There was absolutely no reason for police to have suspected him of being Lynette's killer even if they had known of his temper or use of prostitutes back in 1988. He chose not to provide that assistance on several occasions. Gafoor's account of Lynette's murder simply does not ring true and he has never been challenged over it, because he chose to avoid awkward questions both in interview and at trial.

The Guilty Secret

Police often appeal to murderers to turn themselves in. Unsurprisingly few actually do so. They also ask for help from families of murderers, stressing that they may know something, that killers may have confessed to them, but that, too, rarely solves crimes. After the murder, Gafoor did nothing to betray his guilty secret, but his character underwent changes that in retrospect could have raised flags for those who knew him previously.

He became offended by pornography and the year after the release of the last three members of the Cardiff Five cut himself off from friends and family. He avoided unnecessary human contact to the point of driving three miles to post his rent every week rather than popping it in to his landlord who lived just doors away. It seemed as if he was making sure that he would never find himself in the position where it could happen again and that is also unusual.

Gafoor's only other known offence established that he had a temper, but bore no similarity to the murder. He did not come to police attention for any knife crimes after Lynette's murder and did not develop a blood lust that might have been expected after such a sadistic murder and after his one conviction he avoided social intercourse as much as possible.

For the next decade he did not come to the attention of the police. His behaviour contradicted the expected behaviour of such killers — the murder was unnecessarily brutal, but unlike most sadistic killers Gafoor seemed to be deeply affected by it and determined not to allow himself to be put in a position where such an offence could occur, but that was the limit of his "remorse". Even when working in Germany he kept himself to himself as much as possible. Gradually, he became more and more the loner, but prior to Lynette's murder, while he had few friends and was never the life and soul of the party, he wasn't the recluse that he became. It was impossible to predict that a savage killer would behave in this manner and that is one of the most important lessons of this case. It put offender profiling in the dock.

A Frighteningly Normal but Unusual Killer

Professor Canter's peers might well have produced a similar profile at that time. But how could anyone have possibly predicted a killer with such characteristics as Gafoor possessed? He had no history of mental illness and failed to conform to any of the expected character traits of people capable of such crimes. Most killers are either Caucasian or Asian; Gafoor was both, but that was of little assistance. He was a punter, but that is the end of his predictable character traits and of no real investigative value in itself. The police thoroughly investigated the possibility that Lynette's murderer was a client of hers, but nobody knew or told them that Gafoor used prostitutes, let alone that he used Lynette at least once — the night that he murdered her. He kept that secret to himself.

Beyond the obvious, that the murderer was a punter and that he was likely to be Caucasian or Asian, what did police get from offender profiling in 1988? Knowing that the killer was likely to be white or Asian and that he was likely to be a punter was of no real use at all. You would expect that level of insight from the average amateur sleuth. Gafoor had not graduated from lesser offences through extreme violence until it reached a peak with Lynette's murder and he didn't develop a liking for killing or even violence afterwards. It was also impossible to predict that it would take four years for him to come to police attention after the murder and that police would not hear of him again for another decade when his past caught up with him, not for another violent offence but through DNA. How could this be predicted? And if it can't, then what use is offender profiling in such a case?

Under Fire

So Gafoor is an unusual killer — hopefully a unique one but what if he isn't? Eight years after the Gafoor-effect (that you now have to consider that a particularly brutal killer can have no history of violence or even criminal activity and can revert back to that non-violent personality afterwards)[3] became

---

3. This cycle occurred twice in Gafoor's case, see the description of Gafoor assaulting a work

known there are no newspapers talking about it, or media investigating it (although there was word of a BBC Panorama programme as this book was going to press: though mainly about the collapse of the corruption trial, it seems, and unlikely to deal with the Gafoor effect).

Offender profilers carry on with "run-of-the-mill" profiles, ignoring the possibility that there are other killers like Gafoor out there, but how can they know? Nobody acknowledges this uncomfortable truth. Are there other Gafoors getting away with murder because they don't fit accepted stereotypes? Police forces know how Gafoor was caught due to magnificent work by forensic scientists and by the officers who worked on Operation Mistral (see *Chapter 5* onwards). It was inevitable that offender profiling would fail in the Lynette White case, because Gafoor was the first convicted killer to exhibit these character traits, but now that the possibility has been established, surely it must be acknowledged and incorporated into other investigations.

Nothing, it seems, could account for the entirely new phenomenon that was Jeffrey Gafoor — a killer whose first offence was utterly sadistic, but who was then, so it seems, so shocked and appalled by himself that he took extraordinary steps to prevent repetition. Another prediction that could have been useful was missing from Canter's profile. That the killer would not kill again and would isolate himself from human contact because he deemed it necessary to ensure that he never found himself in the same position again. That would have been a truly invaluable insight into the mind of this killer but how would it have been possible?

Maybe Gafoor's psychological characteristics demand a fundamental rethink of the approach to the investigation of serious crime. Every profile should acknowledge the possibility that the murderer could be another Gafoor, but that would mean accepting that profiling is speculative at best and can be found wanting when it matters most. Not only is it no substitute for real cutting-edge forensic science, but old-fashioned investigative police work can leave it trailing in its wake too. There is nothing perhaps that offender profiling can teach us about the Lynette White case that other forensic science and investigative practices (as conducted by people such as Paul Williams and Dave Barclay: see *Chapter 6*) cannot trump.

---

colleague earlier in the chapter.

The scientific investigations that Barclay and others performed gave Williams the opportunity to shine and he had the wherewithal to allow that evidence to lead him to Gafoor's family and ultimately to Jeffrey Gafoor himself. The Gafoor-effect on offender profiling should therefore serve as a warning. There are killers that don't fit neatly into its boxes. Despite its failings in this case, both police and offender profilers were aware of the need for accountability and have devised a system to deliver it.

Behavioural Investigative Advice

At its best profiling can narrow down lists of likely suspects, but it can also waste police time and resources, especially if profilers get it wrong. Paul Britton's original profile supported Keith Pedder's belief that Colin Stagg was their man. He wasn't — Robert Napper was — and while Stagg was in prison awaiting trial Napper killed again. Professor Canter's profile did not fit Gafoor and at one stage seems to have caused the police to cast attention on an innocent man (*Chapter 10*).

Offender profiling should never amount to anything more than a tool that might assist investigators to concentrate on particular lines of enquiry. As long ago as 1992 it had been noticed that despite being used in 200 cases no research had been conducted to assess how effective it was in the investigation of crime. The Rachel Nickell Inquiry would emphasise that need dramatically. It should never become a substitute for old-fashioned investigation and at least some of the lessons have now been learned and appropriate models developed. About a decade ago offender profiling became known as behavioural investigative advice, which is in many ways a more accurate description of the work that offender profilers do, but it involves far more than just creating profiles of likely offenders.

Police tackled the issue of accountability through accreditation procedures. The Association of Chief Police Officers (ACPO) recognised that the technique had the potential to help police to focus resources on investigating lines of inquiry and even on developing interview strategies. Offender profiling had to be integrated into an approach to investigations that benefitted from other disciplines as well. It has become a far more valuable investigative tool than

133

the one used in the Rachel Nickell and Lynette White investigations, partly because practitioners must be approved by ACPO and their performance is subjected to annual review that can cost them their status if they fall below the required standard. Both the police and behavioural investigative advisers (BIAS) have a clear incentive not to repeat the errors of the past.

ACPO's sub-committee for Behavioural Science is responsible for approving behavioural investigative advisers and their policy, which therefore applies to all police forces in England, Wales and Northern Ireland, only permits advisers approved by ACPO to give such advice. Approved advisers must have their work reviewed every year by an independent panel that has the appropriate qualifications. The panel has the power to remove the adviser from the approved list or renew him or her for another year. The National Crime and Operations Facility (NCOF), which later became the National Policing Improvement Agency (NPIA), runs an organization—the Serious Crime Analysis Section (SCAS)—that works with behavioural investigative advisers. The NPIA also maintains a list of such advisers who have been approved along with ACPO. They provide investigative advice and support to police officers based on behavioural science in the investigation mainly of serious crimes. Among the expertise that they contribute is offender background characteristics, interview strategy and investigative strategies or suggestions.

The NPIA's Crime Operational Support Section employs five behavioural investigative advisers on a regional basis and they are a free resource to police forces. There is no defence equivalent, which is a pity as that would help to guarantee equality of arms and that the evidence of such advisers is adequately reviewed and challenged if necessary. Consequently, behavioural investigative advice, which includes offender profiling, is subject to the necessary quality control that could prevent repetition of the apparent flaws that contributed to the miscarrying of justice in criminal cases, or at least failing to provide the assistance required. Paul Britton is not an accredited BIA, but Professor David Canter is and also trains the next generation of advisers.[4]

---

4. See further www.davidcanter.com There appears to be no mention of the Lynette White inquiry or the "Gaffor effect" at this site (when accessed in May 2012).

CHAPTER 12

TARIFFS — PROTECTING THE GUILTY

The Final Insult

J EFFREY GAFOOR HAD PLEADED GUILTY to the murder of Lynette White. He said that he had acted alone, but despite that he received a lower tariff than the Cardiff Three, so how could that have happened? It is a long story that has its roots in an attempt to free the hands of judges, which failed to achieve that end. It also resulted in another issue that successive governments have ignored; still pretending that there is no problem. It is yet another affront to the ordeal of people shown to be innocent. Mr Justice (Sir John) Royce interpreted and applied the relevant sentencing law in such a way that Gafoor received a tariff of just 13 years before he will become eligible for parole as already noted in *Chapter 1* and further explained in this chapter.

If this was an error, it may have been one that saved Gafoor up to 20 years. Mr Justice Royce set a starting point of 15 years, but seemingly believed that in actual practice this meant starting at 12 years. That was not the approach taken in another notorious Welsh case which happened earlier, but under the same rules, as will be explained. Gafoor won a bonus of three years in any event, arguably winning the lottery because Royce chose not to define his crime as sadistic when the tariff would have started at 30 years. Up to a further ten years could have been added for allowing innocent men to go to jail for his crime. Instead, as noted, Gafoor got a "paltry" 13 years, which was less than the five men whose lives he ruined served in jail in total. Despite this, the Law Commission, Ministry of Justice and all major political parties have declined to alter a loophole that benefits nobody but the truly guilty who allow the innocent to suffer.[1]

---

1. Some further information concerning how the tariff system betrays the innocent are scheduled to appear in a pamphlet "Just Tariffs" (2012) which is to be published in hard copy and possibly in an e-version: see www.fittedin.org.

The Home Secretary Loses the Power to set Tariffs

Until 1999 the minimum term that juvenile murderers must serve in prison before being considered for release (i.e. the tariff) was decided by the Home Secretary. It was a three-stage process. First the trial judge set the amount he or she believed appropriate according to established case law. Then the Lord Chief Justice would consider it and that amount would become the recommendation that was put to the Home Secretary who would then decide on the minimum term that must be served before the convicted murderer could apply to the Parole Board for release on licence. The last phase was always controversial as the Home Secretary is a politician, yet exerted more power over sentencing decisions than judges without possessing their knowledge of the law.

The European Convention on Human Rights (ECHR) entitles all citizens to have their sentences decided by an impartial tribunal which is independent of the government and so the Home Secretary could not be such a tribunal. Although the Convention was drafted by British lawyers, among others, in 1950, Britain did not incorporate the Convention into domestic law until the Human Rights Act 1998.

In December 1999, the European Court of Human Rights (ECtHR) decided that it was unlawful for life sentence prisoners to have their tariffs set by politicians rather than judges and that they were also entitled to a hearing before the judge setting the tariff, but this decision only applied to juveniles for the next three years. The previous system of setting tariffs had lasted 16 years, beginning when the then Home Secretary Leon Brittan announced that the time that the murderer would have to serve in jail had to reflect the need for retribution and deterrence.

Despite being equivalent to the sentencing power of a judge, Parliament gave the power to set tariffs to the Home Secretary, rather than to a tribunal that was independent of government. Prisoners who had been sentenced to life imprisonment and juveniles who had been sentenced to detention at Her Majesty's pleasure had tariffs set by the Home Secretary, but could be detained past their tariff date if they were thought to pose a continued risk to the public.

The law had to be changed to give the power to set tariffs to judges. It took four years and another case coming to the Law Lords[2] on the issue for it to become law through the Criminal Justice Act of 2003 (CJA). Ironically, legislation designed to give sentencing powers back to judges rather than politicians actually succeeded in allowing the executive to tie the hands of judges more effectively than under the previous system.

Tying the Hands of the Judges

In 2002 Anthony Anderson asked the Law Lords to rule that the Home Secretary's power to set tariffs on prisoners serving life was unlawful. Their decision extended the judgement of the ECtHR in *Venables v UK* (which applied to youths)[3] to cover all tariffs,[4] so new legislation was required. The framework of the CJA contains tightly defined starting points (below) and the judge can order a whole life tariff if "the court considers that the seriousness of the offence is exceptionally high and the offender was over 21 when it was committed".

The murder of Lynette White was extremely brutal — sadistic with sexual overtones to it — but it did not meet the criteria for a whole life tariff because there had to be more than one murder to qualify for that. Murders that included the abduction of children could also result in a whole life tariff. Despite its vicious nature, the judge's hands were tied; he could not impose a whole life tariff on Gafoor for Lynette's murder.

If the seriousness of the offence is not considered to be exceptionally high, but was particularly high, the starting point is 30 years. Included here are all the criteria for a whole life tariff if the offender was between 18 and 21 years old and an extra one that applied to the killing of Lynette White — "a murder involving sexual or sadistic conduct". If the facts do not meet those criteria then the appropriate starting point is 15 years if the offender was over 21 (and 12 years if between 18 and 21). After choosing the starting point, the court must then consider aggravating and mitigating circumstances if these have

---

2. In 2009 the Supreme Court took over from the Law Lords as the highest court in the UK.
3. *Venables v United Kingdom* (2000) 30 EHRR 121.
4. *R v Secretary of State for the Home Department, ex parte Anderson* [2002] UKHL 46.

not been taken into account in setting the starting point. There are seven criteria, one of which could have applied to Lynette's murder — "mental or physical suffering inflicted on the victim before death". Alongside considering the aggravating circumstances the court must consider mitigation too. Of seven criteria only a "lack of premeditation" would seem to have applied to Gafoor, although the CJA does not prevent previous convictions and timely guilty pleas from being taken into account.

Gafoor's Tariff

Jeffrey Gafoor was sentenced to life imprisonment on July 4th 2003; the judge could do no less as that is the mandatory sentence for murder. "You allowed innocent men to go to prison for a crime that you knew you had committed," he told Gafoor. He also said that he viewed this as the most important aggravating circumstance, even though it was not specifically included in the CJA, or any other case law for that matter. This was, after all, the first time that it had happened in British legal history in a case affected by the 2003 Act. Nevertheless, a deterrent tariff might have been expected as not only was this the most brutal crime of its type in Welsh history at the time,[5] but Gafoor had also allowed five innocent men to spend a total of 16 years in prison. It had ruined their lives, that of their families and also those of Lynette's family. It therefore required the harshest possible tariff that the law permitted.

In October 2005, Mr Justice Royce set out his reasoning for the minimum term that Gafoor must serve before he, Gafoor, would be eligible for release on parole. He chose a starting point of 15 years, but did not explain why the seriousness of the crime was not particularly high on the grounds of its apparent sadistic and sexual content (see further below) and also because of the effect that the miscarriage of justice had had on all of the victims and public confidence in the CJS. Then he turned to aggravating circumstances. "I regard it as a very serious aggravating factor; the fact that he was content

---

5. Twenty-six-year-old shipping clerk Geraldine Palk was raped, stabbed 81 times and bludgeoned to death as well by Mark Hampson on December 22nd, 1990.

to allow innocent men to be arrested, to stand their trial and be convicted of a murder he knew he had committed," said Royce. "Furthermore it was accepted on his behalf that those men notwithstanding their release by the Court of Appeal had been stigmatised over the ensuing years." The scientific evidence and other evidence proved that they were innocent and Gafoor alone was guilty. He then moved on to other aggravating circumstances. "I also regard it as an aggravating factor that the body was hacked so terribly and so frequently," said the judge. "It verged on the sadistic. It was also of note that he had taken a knife with him that night, it was said for his own protection."

Why did that crime "verge" on the sadistic? The description of it that Royce himself gave leaves no doubt that it *was* sadistic. "She had been savagely killed," said Royce:

> Her throat had a massive diagonal cut from the right ear across the front and around the left side beneath the angle of the jaw, exposing the bones of the spine. Her breasts and chest area had 25 stab wounds. There were many other wounds to the face, stomach, arms, wrists and left thigh. The total wounds exceeded 50. There were defensive wounds to the hands, indicating resistance.

Clearly, the level of violence that Lynette suffered was far beyond what was required to subdue or even kill her. If such a degree of brutality does not make the seriousness of the offence particularly high, there are grave problems with the definition itself. The murder had sexual overtones to it and there were other problems as well. In my view it was utterly sadistic and the tariff should have reflected that with a starting point of 30 years. By not considering the savagery of the attack in setting the starting point, the judge could only take it into account in the aggravating circumstances and there are limits on the amount that can be set for that even if there are other serious aggravating factors as there were in this case. So all in all, the punishment did not fit the crime.

Royce believed that under Schedule 21 of the 2003 Act the appropriate starting point was 15 years and that was the figure he used to calculate aggravating circumstances and mitigation before deciding on the final tariff. Royce found two major aggravating factors. The first was that Gafoor was prepared to allow men he knew to be innocent to suffer wrongful imprisonment for his crime. The other was the brutality of the attack. Schedule 21 to the CJA and subsequent case law does not cater for a killer allowing innocent people to be accused and convicted of his crime, so Mr Justice Royce had arguably exceeded his powers by taking that into account at all, yet there was to be another surprise. "I conclude that these aggravating factors justify an increase from the 15 year starting point to nineteen-and-a-half years," he said. He hadn't imposed the maximum allowed for aggravating circumstances which would have meant a tariff of 20 years. Why not? Arguably, the sheer brutality of the murder alone deserved the maximum, but Gafoor had also allowed innocent men to wrongfully spend a total of 16 years in prison for his crime as well. If that combination does not deserve the maximum amount possible being added for aggravating circumstances, what does?

After setting the term for aggravating circumstances, Royce had to consider mitigating factors. Gafoor only had one previous conviction, for unlawful wounding, in 1992. His legal team commissioned a psychiatric report to determine whether he would present a danger in the future, yet declined to put it before the judge. Royce considered the victim impact statements, where Lynette's family detailed the effect that her murder had had upon them. Royce found them very moving, but there were other victims in this case that were denied the opportunity to detail the effect that it had had on them—the Cardiff Five and their families. They should have been given the same courtesy, especially as the judge considered what happened to them to be the most important aggravating circumstance. Excluding them in these circumstances made no sense and denied the impact of their victimisation.

"The maximum discount for a plea of guilty to murder is one sixth if made at the first reasonable opportunity," said Royce. "Although [Gafoor] had admitted the killing he had refused to answer other questions in interview about the circumstances. There is also material now before me confirming that the defendant post-sentence gave some assistance to the police in their investigation of how it came to be that innocent men were convicted of Lynette White's murder."

The guilty plea was the strongest mitigating factor amounting to two years and six months. His assistance to police in the inquiry into the original Lynette White Inquiry provided some as well, but Gafoor had ample opportunity to own up to his crime. Fifteen years had passed between the murder and his arrest. He made no attempt to take responsibility for his crime or to confess to anyone. When police officers knocked on his door to ask for a sample for DNA-testing, his reply showed that he still sought to evade responsibility. "Haven't you got somebody for that?" he asked.

Then he went on to try to provide a false explanation for his DNA being found at the crime scene before giving a sample for testing. Gafoor could have acknowledged his guilt then, but chose to try to cheat justice by attempting to take his own life. He had the opportunity to give a small crumb of comfort to both Lynette White's family and the Cardiff Five and their families by taking responsibility early and explaining what had happened to Lynette, but took the cowardly and selfish option every time. He accepted responsibility on the way to hospital when he hoped to die. He didn't die and had the opportunity to admit his guilt during interviews with police. Instead, he made no comment and left the police to prove their case, which they did.

He pleaded guilty, but that was 15 years too late. It cannot erase the pain and guilt of Lynette's family or the suffering and stigma endured by the Cardiff Five and their families. It was too little, too late and the tariff should have reflected that. Only Gafoor could have prevented them from losing a total of 16 years of their lives as he knew for certain that all five were innocent. He alone could have proved it, unequivocally, but chose to get on with his life knowing that he had allowed innocent men to pay for his crime. Nevertheless, even in these circumstances, the law credits him for pleading guilty swiftly, what is known as a timely guilty plea. Why? This was not a guilty plea at the first reasonable opportunity, hardly timely at all; it came when he had little choice as the evidence had left him no hiding place. There were other less important factors that Gafoor relied on in mitigation too.

"I accept that this murder was not pre-planned," said Royce. "However he had gone out, unlawfully, with a knife in part because he said he had been robbed by prostitutes. He clearly contemplated he might resort to using it in a confrontation with a prostitute. He was a relatively young man with no previous convictions at the time. These matters provide some but not much mitigation."

Royce had to evaluate all these mitigating factors. He allowed four years, but appears to have subsequently miscalculated when applying it to crimes committed before 2002, which he believed compelled him to arrive at a final starting point of 12 years, rather than the 15 he used to calculate the aggravating and mitigating circumstances as mentioned earlier in this chapter.

He believed that he had to take the lower of the two figures in deciding the final starting point for the number of years to be imposed. However, two other Welsh cases suggest otherwise. Both Geraldine Palk and Karen Skipper were murdered before 2002 and Mark Hampson was convicted of Palk's murder before the CJA became law in 2003 (as Gafoor was). Despite this Mrs Justice (Dame Heather, now Lady Justice) Hallett imposed a 20 year tariff from a 15 year starting point with full aggravating circumstances and no mitigation at all. Mr Justice (Sir Nigel) Davis set a tariff of 19 years on John Pope in 2009 for the 1996 murder of Karen Skipper, which meant a 15 year starting point as well, so Royce too could have applied the 15 year starting point rather than the 12 year one that he did.

"If I took a starting point of 12 years and increased it by four and a half years for aggravating factors I would then reduce it to 13 years to take account of mitigating factors including the plea," said Royce. "It would then be appropriate to deduct the time spent in custody on remand which is just short of four months. This produces a term of 12 years and eight months." But are there not flaws in this reasoning? Having previously allowed four years for mitigation, the judge deducted three years and six months in his final calculations. Gafoor, of course, had little cause for complaint: he should have received a much longer term.

Sadism

The public's understanding of the word "sadistic" appears vastly different from that of some judges. Lynette White's throat had been slit to the spine. That Gafoor continued to stab her after death was certain. There were sexual overtones to the killing and Gafoor sought the services of a prostitute, nobody forced him to do so and nobody made him kill his victim in such a vicious manner. That was his choice. Sadism, as far as the public is concerned, includes sexually motivated violence and cruelty. Sexual gratification is harder to prove in Gafoor's case as his reaction at the time was known only by him, but even if it was not clear, any reasonable person would consider his crime to be sadistic and, consequently, it should have been treated as such. Gafoor stabbed his victim's breasts. Why? This was not designed to kill. It was intended to sexually maim. It was surely sadistic, yet Royce claimed that it "verged on the sadistic". This begs the question of what degree of violence is required to qualify as sadistic.

Ronald Castree was convicted of the murder of eleven-year-old Lesley Molseed 32 years after he killed her. A terrible miscarriage of justice occurred in-between-times, Mr Justice (Sir Peter) Openshaw told Castree that he would have to serve a minimum of 30 years imprisonment because of the seriousness of that crime. It shows that Openshaw regarded it as particularly serious. Castree was denied leave to appeal in 2010 against both his conviction and the tariff. Delivering the Court of Appeal judges' decision, Lord Justice (Sir David) Latham said: "This was without doubt a horrific murder. The sexual violence was not of the worst kind, but the actual killing was a savage attack with a knife. It merits the most severe punishment".

So why did they fail to add aggravating circumstances and why does this not apply to the murder of Lynette White? Lynette was not a child, but she was young and the violence that she suffered was even worse. There were more stabbings and the sexual violence was of a terrible kind. The starting point should have been 30 years on that basis and the aggravating circumstances should then have been used in full for allowing innocent men to go to prison, resulting in a tariff of around 33 years.

Why did the CPS fail to appeal against the leniency of the tariff imposed on Gafoor? It is useful to consider what Sir Nigel Davis said in Pope's case. He described the murder of Karen Skipper in the following terms. "This wasn't simply callous," Davis said, "It seems to me that it was almost sadistic". What does it take for judges to define a murder as sadistic? She had been stabbed, stripped of her jeans and underwear and then been thrown into the River Ely to drown. It was a horrible way to die. It was cruel and plainly had elements of sexual gratification. Why was this almost sadistic rather than sadistic? Had Davis given that label to the murder, his starting point could have been 30 years and then he could have considered the other aggravating circumstances, that the offender showed no remorse and allowed an innocent man to stand trial.

The attack on Geraldine Palk is impossible to conceive of as anything but sadistic. She was raped, bludgeoned and stabbed repeatedly, although the pathologist found no evidence of rape or genital mutilation, which was said to be a characteristic of a sex-related killing. Nevertheless, semen contributed to identifying Hampson as her killer, as his defence of consensual sexual activity was rejected by the jury. He had subjected her to a two-minute-long attack of staggering viciousness. "You're in my judgement a vicious and wicked man," Mrs Justice Hallett told Hampson on conviction. "During the trial, I didn't detect the slightest hint of remorse from you." Hallett also described the crime as "A sadistic and sexually motivated crime that devastated a community".

Hallett considered the tariff that she could set. She was disappointed that she could not set a higher tariff than the 20 years that she set in January 2006. "If I had the power to increase the minimum term to be served in the light of current statutory provisions, I would do so," said Hallett. "Given the circumstances of the murder and his record of violence, I have my doubts as to whether it will ever be safe to release him." She found no mitigating circumstances at all, but given her comments on the sadistic nature of the offence it is surprising that she did not use that to set a starting point of 30 years. However, it is a moot point now. Hampson died in prison in December 2007.

There has been criticism of the tactics employed by Hampson's defence lawyers during the four week trial in Bristol, John Charles Rees QC putting Palk's character on trial by probing aspects of her life and sexual history. They insisted that this approach was legitimate as they had to present their client's case as strongly as possible, but Hallett was seemingly unimpressed and Palk's brother, Neil, wondered whether at times Geraldine herself was the one on trial. Hampson's protestations of innocence fell on deaf ears and he lost his appeal. The murder of Geraldine Palk was a brutal and horrific crime that was quite rightly labelled "sadistic", but Lynette White's murder was also sadistic without being termed that and there were further matters in that case that demand attention.

An Inappropriate System

There are several issues that arise regarding the minimum term that murderers like Gafoor should serve. Gafoor received a lower tariff than the Cardiff Three had imposed on them. That is an insult to every concept of justice. Gafoor can do all of the courses and express remorse for his crime, as he has something to be sorry about. In prison, the Cardiff Three would have been asked to provide details of the crime — details they did not know and could not invent convincingly, especially as the verdict contradicted even the prosecution case. The CJS placed them in an absurd position that punished them for being innocent. That was bad enough, but on top of that they were then forced to watch helplessly along with Lynette White's family as Gafoor was rewarded by the same system for not only being guilty but for callously watching while the lives of all of the victims of this case were destroyed.

As already noted, Gafoor received a tariff of just 12 years and eight months. That is considerably less than the Cardiff Five jointly served in prison for Gafoor's crime. The system rewarded the guilty at the expense of the innocent. How can this be justified? Even though South Wales Police and Mr Justice Royce acknowledge that the Cardiff Five are victims of the CJS, there is no law prohibiting what Gafoor did to them. He did not perjure himself, or conspire to pervert the course of justice; he simply stayed quiet when he alone knew that innocent men were having their lives ruined for his crime, so Royce had to negotiate a legal minefield. There were no precedents that he could apply to this situation and his hands were tied by the very legislation that was designed to make sentencing decisions on life sentence prisoners the domain of judges, but the framework did not cater for this situation — a circumstance that nobody had predicted. However, there is a problem with that interpretation.

The CJA became law on November 20th 2003, four-and-a-half months after it was known that Gafoor had allowed innocent men to suffer a total of 16 years of extremely damaging wrongful incarceration. There is therefore no excuse for legislation failing to take into account that murderers who allow the innocent to suffer for their crimes should be punished for that when the minimum term that they should serve is determined. All it required was recognition that this is an aggravating circumstance in its own right in Schedule 21 to the 2003 Act. It could also have led to a change in that schedule, allowing judges to set the amounts to be calculated for aggravating and mitigating circumstances according to the facts of the case being considered. There is no good reason to have rigid guidelines that prevent judges setting appropriate tariffs according to the circumstances of individual cases as happened in this case. Only the truly guilty that allow the innocent to suffer for their murders have anything to fear from legislation that takes it into account in this manner.

Nevertheless, there are in my view problems with Mr Justice Royce's approach as I have already explained. The murder of Lynette White didn't "verge" on the sadistic — it was sadistic! The seriousness of the offence was particularly high because the murder involved sadistic and sexual conduct, so the starting point should therefore have been 30 years and if, somehow, such an horrific murder was not deemed to be sadistic enough, how could the facts not deserve the full five years that Royce could have applied for aggravating circumstances? The CJA does not have an aggravating factor to cater for what Gafoor did to the Cardiff Five and nor did previous case law. This was acknowledged by Royce when setting the minimum term that Gafoor must serve when quoting a judgement given by Lord Bingham, the then Lord Chief Justice. "His examples of aggravating factors do not include what I regard as the most serious aggravating factor in this case namely allowing innocent men to be convicted of the murder," said Royce. "That is hardly surprising as it is such an unusual feature."

However, Royce included it anyway, but there was no discretion for judges within Schedule 21, nor in case law, to take that into account. Consequently, Royce had no real authority to consider what Gafoor had done to the Cardiff Five as an aggravating circumstance under the current system, i.e. under that schedule, yet he did so anyway. It might have been better if he hadn't, as that would have demonstrated the iniquity in the current system conclusively and possibly forced the government to act. Instead the Law Commission was able to claim that there was no loophole that needed closing and refused to recommend that a future Criminal Justice Act reflects this. The result is that other murderers who allow the innocent to suffer do not pay for what they have done to the wrongly accused. Shamefully, it didn't end there. The Ministry of Justice was also given an opportunity to close the loophole and it too declined to do so. The change to a Coalition government in 2010 made no difference either.

Preventing Miscarriages of Justice

Murderers who allow innocent people to suffer for their crimes are arguably the most contemptible criminals of all. They deserve to be dealt with severely, including serving an additional amount of time in prison for the damage they have done to the innocent. Alternatively, such conduct should be made into a separate criminal offence with, in the case of murder, an additional sentence to be served consecutively with the tariff for murder. However, if someone helps to prevent a miscarriage of justice, then as with a timely guilty plea, they should be rewarded with time off if they can prove their assistance in solving the crime. It only requires a change in the law to explicitly acknowledge the possibility that this can and does happen and either to include it as an aggravating circumstance, or make it a separate offence that carries its own penalty if the offender allows it to happen — and a mitigating circumstance if they help to prevent a miscarriage of justice.

The Ministry of Justice refuses to implement this suggestion, claiming that it is too complicated. Consequently all political parties remain soft on the most unscrupulous of murderers that not only involve a killing but allow innocent people to go to jail. This despite the fact that advances in forensic science have made it inevitable that the Cardiff Five will not be the last people to be fully vindicated in Britain.

As with Gafoor, the suffering of the innocent has not been taken into account except verbally. In August 2006, after a retrial, Rickie and Danny Preddie were convicted of the manslaughter of ten-year-old Damilola Taylor. The young boy had been stabbed in the leg and left to bleed to death in November 2000. Four juveniles were either acquitted by the jury or on the orders of Mr Justice (Sir Anthony, now Lord Justice) Hooper at their trial in 2002.

The Preddies were aged 12 and 13 when Taylor died, so they were sentenced accordingly to eight years youth custody by Mr Justice (Sir John) Goldring, even though both had become adults by October 2006. Taylor's father,

Richard, derided the sentences as not deterring other criminals, but there was another problem with it. The Preddie brothers had allowed four boys to stand trial for their crime four years earlier, but not a single day of their sentence will be for the time served on remand by those boys who had been wrongly accused and the effect that it had on their lives. Yet again, the law ignored the guilty, allowing the innocent to suffer wrongful imprisonment even though no convictions were obtained in that case. Their incarceration on remand was still a miscarriage of justice and this case illustrates another problem with the tariff system. There was no mechanism whatsoever to take into account the Preddie's allowing five others to stand trial for their crime. Hassan Jihad was acquitted of all charges at the first trial in April 2006 that resulted in a hung jury on the manslaughter charges against the Preddies. Unlike Gafoor, the Preddie brothers were children when they allowed the four youths to stand trial for their crime.

It had happened again, yet there was still no recognition of the problem, let alone solution. Not only were killers not punished for allowing the innocent to suffer for their crimes, but they were encouraged to take their chances by the indifference of all major political parties and this time it proved beyond doubt that change was needed. Manslaughter does not result in a tariff. Consequently, there was absolutely nothing that Goldring could do about it. He could not order the Preddies to serve so much as one day in jail for allowing five others to risk wrongful imprisonment. Unsurprisingly, it was not long before it happened again.

Thirty-two years after the murder of eleven-year-old Lesley Molseed, Ronald Castree was brought to justice. But even the 30 year tariff on Castree does not fully deliver justice. Molseed's family says that she can rest in peace now that Castree will spend at least 30 years behind bars for her murder, but what about Stefan Kiszko and his campaigning mother Charlotte? Can they rest in peace with a tariff that does not recognise that they too are victims of Castree? Molseed's murder was a dreadful crime, but so was allowing an innocent man to lose 16 years of his life for that crime, and Kiszko would lose his life for good within a year of his release. Where was the recognition of Castree's role in Kiszko's suffering? Kiszko was a second victim of Castree's crime. Four years after Gafoor's conviction this proved that the law was still in serious need of change as the ordeal of another vindicated person was ignored. Mr Justice Openshaw's starting point shows that he had not added anything for aggravating circumstances.

There are further examples. In December 2008, one of Britain's most shameful miscarriages of justice was finally correctly resolved. Colin Stagg was always entirely innocent of the horrific 1992 murder of Rachel Nickell, despite standing trial two years later. Robert Napper was the real killer. He is detained in Broadmoor indefinitely for the 1993 manslaughters of Samantha and Jazmine Bissett. He suffered from an abnormality of personality that the cps acknowledged influenced his actions in 1992. Napper is undoubtedly a very dangerous man and it took a long time for him to acknowledge that he had killed Rachel Nickell, although his responsibility was diminished. Napper's psychiatric condition mitigates some responsibility for allowing Stagg to stand trial for his crime, but as with the Preddies there was no means of taking into account that Napper had done so. But Gafoor and Castree have no excuse for allowing the innocent to suffer for their crimes and nor did John Pope mentioned earlier in this chapter. In February 2009, he was convicted of the March 1996 murder of Karen Skipper while she was walking her dogs. Her hands were bound behind her back with the dogs' leads and after being forcibly undressed from below the waist, she was thrown into the river Ely in Cardiff, in which she drowned. Her estranged husband Phillip stood trial in 1997 and was acquitted. He died of stomach cancer in 2004, aged just 48 without seeing Pope convicted. Mr Justice Davis described Pope as a "devious" man and told him, "This wasn't simply callous. It seems to me that it was almost sadistic." Pope was then told that he would have to serve a minimum of 19 years imprisonment.

"It is difficult to think but that you were hoping that he would be convicted, because if he were convicted, then the real truth would never thereafter emerge." Davis continued, "This is an old offence but that is because you have evaded justice for so long." He pointed out that Pope's conviction proved that Skipper was an innocent man: "It is owed to the memory of him that this be publicly stated."

But apparently his memory does not require his ordeal be taken into account in setting an appropriate tariff. Given Davis' belief that it was almost sadistic and had sexual overtones to it, the aggravating circumstances could only account for five years. That may have included allowing Phillip Skipper to stand trial as well. He had no mitigation worthy of the name, but the full amount permitted was not added to the starting point. Yet again the tariff system had been found wanting when dealing with vindication.[6]

Despite five cases of vindication, the Ministry of Justice does not believe that there is a problem, let alone the need to resolve it. A sixth made no difference either although David Lace was different. Sean Hodgson is the longest serving victim of a miscarriage of justice in Britain. Convicted of the 1979 rape and murder of Teresa di Simone, Hodgson lost nearly three decades of his life. He was cleared by DNA in 2009 and Lace's remains were exhumed. DNA confirmed Lace's guilt, but unlike all the others Lace had tried to take responsibility for his crime by confessing shortly after Hodgson's conviction, but was not believed and later committed suicide. Had he lived to stand trial his case would have been unique — the only murderer to try to take responsibility rapidly and deserve it to be taken into account in mitigation.

The innocent are entitled to be protected from wrongful accusations if at all possible. But, if that proves impossible, their victimhood needs to be acknowledged. Knowingly allowing the innocent to suffer wrongful imprisonment, whether convicted or not, should carry a penalty. Either the law should be changed to criminalise such conduct or it should be an independent aggravating factor that judges are free to employ according to the merits of the particular case being considered, without limits, and in addition to other factors, although the circumstances of the Damilola Taylor and Rachel Nickell cases also suggest that new legislation is required. It is seemingly at present a lottery that depends on the interpretation of individual judges as to what the starting point should be or whether allowing the innocent to be convicted or held in custody should even be included as an aggravating circumstance. Even so, the Law Commission, Ministry of Justice and all major political parties think nothing needs to be done.

---

6. In 2010 Pope won a retrial, which took place in June and July 2011. He was convicted again after having attempted to turn the events into yet another retrial of Phillip Skipper, but without the inconvenience of the burden of proof. The prosecution, led by Ian Murphy QC, did not adequately prove Skipper to be innocent. Pope was convicted again. Murphy did not ask for a higher tariff and the judge, Mr Justice (Sir Roderick) Evans imposed the same one as before without commenting on the fact that Pope was content to allow an innocent man to stand trial for his crime and ruin the lives of that man's family.

The Most Important Factor

Allocating additional time for aggravating circumstances in the Lynette White case simply did not do justice to what had happened. In fact it was an insult to every concept of justice that such serious aggravating factors as existed in that case only outweighed comparatively trivial mitigation by a year. That alone shows that the whole issue of tariffs, especially in cases where innocent people have been wrongfully accused, must be looked at again and justice delivered to the innocent as well as the victim's family. Lynette White, her family, the Cardiff Five and their families are all victims of Gafoor's sadistic crime and his long silence. Mr Justice Royce did not stick to the 15 year starting point, even though Gafoor's conviction came later than Hampson's. The CPS also failed to appeal against the leniency of the tariffs in both cases. It was therefore arguably at fault in both instances.

Mr Justice Royce also believed that the fact that Jeffrey Gafoor allowed men he knew to be innocent to serve a total of 16 years imprisonment for a crime that he knew he had committed to be the most important aggravating circumstance, yet the tariff that he chose to set did not seem to reflect that. It also did not reflect the fact that in 1988 it was the most sadistic murder of its type in Welsh history. While his hands were tied by legislation in terms of the tariff that he could set, there was more discretion than perhaps he had realised. The CJS owes the wrongly accused recognition of their suffering and this should be reflected in the tariffs imposed on murderers who knowingly allow the innocent to suffer for their crimes. It should also be acknowledged by public recognition of the power of vindication as a force for change as I will demonstrate further in the next chapter.

CHAPTER 13

THE POWER OF VINDICATION

A Potent Weapon for the Innocent

DNA-TESTING HAS FUNDAMENTALLY CHANGED THE CJS, offering powerful evidence of guilt, but even more so of innocence. For every crime that it has helped to clear up by pointing the police in the right direction, it has proved hundreds or even thousands of people innocent by eliminating them as the source of DNA at a crime scene. It has also helped to prove that people were wrongly convicted in older cases in many jurisdictions beyond our own. There is no reason why it cannot continue to do that as long as testing is conducted whenever required. The Criminal Cases Review Commission (CCRC) uses it, especially in old cases, but the CCRC lacks the resources and indeed the need to vindicate. The CCRC's function is to refer a case back for appeal if it believes there is a real possibility that the Court of Appeal would intervene. It is not there to try to prove innocence.

Applicants to the CCRC can ask it to conduct DNA-testing, but they can't force it to do so. They have the option of judicial review to compel it to do so, but this hardly ever succeeds. Nevertheless, even in cases where DNA is not an issue, juries demand DNA evidence, which is a consequence of believing drama to be fact—the "CSI" effect. DNA is not left at every crime scene, so it is not useful in every case, but an integrated approach to scientific disciplines works wonders. It can indicate whether DNA-testing is likely to yield significant results and if, after review, such testing is likely to produce useful results, of course it should be conducted. While the failure to find DNA is not proof of innocence in every case, it could at least affect the case scenario, which should be revised on an evidence-led basis whenever required. Rigid adherence to a case hypothesis is likely to prove disastrous and has contributed to miscarriages of justice. Properly validated forensic science is an essential tool for justice, but interpretation of evidence is very important too. Forensic science can and has disproved case hypotheses, but instead of that resulting in investigations of different lines of inquiry, the science is challenged, or fanciful explanations provided to claim the results cannot be relied on after all. Both prosecutors and defence lawyers are guilty of this and it has resulted in injustice.

Even after a conviction has been quashed or a defendant has been acquitted, DNA-testing can still have a part to play. The National DNA Database has generated new lines of inquiry in such cases and in some it has resolved those crimes after miscarriages of justice vindicating the original defendants. However, this is rare as the CJS has little to gain and much to lose by vindicating the innocent, because it highlights errors unequivocally. Nevertheless, the truth has a tendency to emerge and in the cases where this occurs the damage done to the integrity of the system is far greater than if the nettle had been grasped promptly. Vindication offers a new opportunity to learn from the past, correct mistakes and improve the CJS for the future. It is the most potent weapon for justice ever and it happened even before DNA-testing was a twinkle in the eye of the innocent, or the guilty for that matter, resulting in major changes to the CJS. For example, the infamous Maxwell Confait Inquiry in the 1970s demonstrated both the dangers of a closed mind to evidence, but also the power of vindication.

End of An Era

In the early hours of April 22nd 1972, firemen discovered the body of 26 year-old mixed-race transvestite, Maxwell Confait, in his abode in South-East London. He had been beaten and strangled and an accelerant had been used in the fire, although the fire would prove to be the red herring that helped to cause a grave miscarriage of justice. The investigation was extremely flawed and belonged to an era when police attitudes towards this type of victim—Confait was a male prostitute as well as the victim of a terrible miscarriage of justice—fell far below acceptable standards. Public antipathy towards both the victim of the crime and those wrongfully accused, helped to facilitate a preventable travesty of justice. The forensic pathology was a complete mess as well and played a large part in the miscarriage that followed, but attitudes had to change throughout the CJS in order to avoid a recurrence and that would take the best part of a decade. Eventually, it would result in two major pieces of legislation that provided safeguards designed to prevent repetition, the Police and Criminal Evidence Act 1984 (PACE) and the Crown Prosecution Service (CPS).

It also contributed to a greater understanding of the responsibilities of forensic scientists. Professor James Cameron estimated that Confait's death occurred between 7.45 am and 11.45 am, while the police surgeon Angus Bain said that it was between 8.00 am and 10.00 am. Both were wrong by some distance and would have cause to want to forget their roles in this embarrassing inquiry. Both Bain and Cameron took a decision not to take rectal temperature, which was a standard procedure at the time, in order to avoid interfering with evidence of sexual activity. This was unlikely to have happened anyway and it was long before DNA-testing was routinely conducted. Cameron said that the body was cold to touch and that rigor mortis had just set in — actually it was departing, which meant that Bain and Cameron had got the time of death badly wrong and that made a mess of the alibi evidence and the investigation.

Confait had been strangled with a piece of wire cut from a lamp, both of which were found in his room. Winston Goode, Confait's landlord, was a credible suspect, but police rapidly lost interest in him and he was not Confait's murderer. He subsequently committed suicide in 1974 by taking cyanide. There was a spate of arson on Monday April 24th 1972, the weekend after the fire at Doggett Road, Catford, which had been Confait's home. These fires were nearby and the significance seemed obvious. A vulnerable 18-year-old, Colin Lattimore, was quickly apprehended. He accepted that he was responsible for the three fires that had been set that day. Understandably, he was then asked about the one at Confait's home and said that he had lit it with Ronald Leighton, but that they had put it out and left it smoking when they left. That should still have rung alarm bells. If the fire was out, but smoking when they left, why was the fire brigade called and why did it require their attention to extinguish it? Those alarm bells should quickly have become a deafening din as the fire had nothing to do with Confait's murder, but Cameron got the time of death horribly wrong. He was not the only distinguished forensic pathologist to do so, but there were other issues that would also be addressed later, including the police bullying admissions from children.

Bullying of Children

Leighton and his friend Ahmet Salih were aged 15 and 14 respectively at the time. Lattimore was an adult, but had the IQ of an eight-year-old. Superintendent Alan Jones and detective inspector Graham Stockwell interviewed them that day without adequate support, which breached the Judges' Rules,[1] because they were under-age and entitled to the protection of an appropriate adult. They rapidly confessed. Leighton and Lattimore admitted the murder and arson and in Leighton's case a burglary too. Salih admitted the arson charge and burglary too, but he did not confess to murder—just that he had been there watching. All three were charged accordingly and remanded in custody. Salih's confession was not signed until a Turkish interpreter could be found, who was the closest thing to an appropriate adult that occurred in this wretched case.

The police had found three vulnerable suspects. Even in the 1970s children were entitled to be interviewed in the presence of a parent or guardian or, in their absence, an adult of the same sex who was not a police officer. It didn't happen, but there was a loophole. The law only demanded that as far as was practicable. Police were left to decide whether it was or not and they didn't have to worry at the time; it could be tested in court later after the interviews had been conducted and confessions obtained. The three boys had no appropriate adult present during their interviews. They claimed that they had been beaten by police into confessing. Nevertheless, the murder charge against Salih was dropped on June 2nd and he was released on bail.

The prosecution, which started on November 1st before Mr Justice Chapman, was shameful. Their case was that Salih had stood in the doorway, watching, while Leighton and Lattimore strangled Confait. Lattimore and Salih accused detective constable Peter Woledge of assaulting them and

---

1. The Judges' Rules was the standard that governed police-related evidence gathering procedures at that time. They were subsequently replaced by PACE, largely due to this case.

Leighton said that he had been pushed around. All three had alibis for the times presented by the pathologist, but Cameron undermined that when giving evidence by saying that the fire could have sped up the onset of rigor mortis and that death could have occurred as late as 1.00 pm. Taking rectal temperature to estimate time of death was a flawed technique, even though that didn't happen in this case—something that was well known even then. Moving the time of death effectively ambushed the defence, as they had prepared their cases based on the previous account that Cameron had given. It would later prove to be utterly incompetent forensic pathology, but not just by Cameron.

On November 24th 1972 the ambush succeeded in securing a shameful miscarriage of justice. All three were convicted as charged apart from Lattimore, who was found guilty of manslaughter due to diminished responsibility. This was not the CJS's finest hour. On July 23rd 1973 an application for leave to appeal was dismissed. Lord Justice (Sir Nigel, later Baron) Bridge delivered the judgement, having found no grounds to interfere with the jury's verdict.

Two courts had therefore implicitly rejected accusations of police malpractice. This illustrated grave failings throughout the CJS as the police had actually trampled the Judges' Rules under foot. This would later be acknowledged by the Court of Appeal, a judicial inquiry and a Royal Commission, so how was it missed by Chapman and Bridge? It was further evidence that the judiciary did not understand vulnerabilities and how to enforce the Rule of Law in such circumstances. The police had "got away" with such methods previously and they knew they were effective. Why would they abandon tried and tested methods, especially when the judiciary failed to put them straight? Sadly this is a lesson that still requires repetition.

The Presumption of Guilt

Lattimore's father, George, began a campaign and secured allies, including the future MP Christopher Price, who would later write an important book on the case.[2] The Director of Public Prosecutions (DPP) and the government were informed of the allegations of assault, but were not interested. Nevertheless, the campaign gathered pace after the change of government in 1974. Two more noted forensic pathologists of the day, Donald Teare and Keith Simpson stated with certainty that death had occurred no later than 10.30 pm on the night of the fire. They were both right, but their opinions were embarrassingly far from accurate as well. Nevertheless, Teare appeared in a documentary in November 1974 repeating his view. Confait had not died later than the time they said; he had died many hours earlier.

The change in government proved important. Price took over from Carol Johnson as the local MP — both supported Lattimore's campaign, which helped to convince the Home Secretary, Roy Jenkins, to refer the convictions back for appeal on June 18th 1975. Lord Justice (Sir Leslie) Scarman, who later became a Law Lord, sat with Lord Justice (Sir Roger) Ormrod and Mr Justice (Sir Graham) Swanwick in that appeal, which began on October 17th, 1975. They quashed the convictions as unsafe and unsatisfactory, mainly due to the pathology evidence having fallen apart. Their judgement criticised police conduct as well, but there had been failures by all parts of the CJS including the lawyers. Retired judge Sir Henry Fisher was appointed to chair an inquiry, although it excluded the conduct of the lawyers and Fisher had conditions of his own. He insisted on the right to determine guilt on the balance of probabilities and got it, despite it being an outrageous concession that resulted in a thoroughly unjustified whispering campaign against Leighton and Salih and subsequently damaged Fisher's reputation.

Assistant chief constable John Fryer of West Mercia Police conducted a review for the Fisher Inquiry and seemingly got it wrong, claiming that there was no evidence against any then living person other than the three original defendants. Fisher followed his lead, rejecting the serious accusations of police malpractice, but accepting that there had been breaches of the rules. Fisher recommended that interviews should be tape-recorded for confessions to be admissible. However, he ignored the scientific evidence, which, based on the evidence then available, established that the murder

---

2. *The Confait Confessions* (1997), Christopher Price and Jonathan Caplan, London: Marion Boyars.

took place at a time when Lattimore was strongly alibied by 23 witnesses. Fisher then reached the completely wrong conclusion that Leighton and Salih were probably guilty. Whatever happened to the much vaunted restoration of the presumption of innocence?

There was no scientific evidence that tied any of the three to Confait or his home. If Lattimore's alibi was accepted then his confession could not be relied on. The breaches of the Judges' Rules suggested that he had told the truth about his treatment as well. His confession was therefore unreliable and exposed police malpractice, so how could the other confessions be relied on when they had been obtained in a similar fashion? There was, in fact, no evidence at all that could justify this conclusion. Fisher's inquiry took two years to report and resulted in some amendment of the Judges' Rules, but more was required on a number of fronts before root and branch change occurred. Lattimore, Leighton and Salih had to be vindicated first and that required a Royal Commission and the will to investigate thoroughly.

A Change is Gonna Come

The Royal Commission on Criminal Procedure 1979-81 had to clear the conduct of the three all over again and improve procedures as well. Among the matters it considered was whether interviews with suspects should be tape-recorded. It was chaired by Sir Cyril Phillips[3] and remains one of the most important contributions ever in terms of the administration of justice in England and Wales. The Police and Criminal Evidence Act 1984 was the legislation that replaced the discredited Judges' Rules and governed the treatment of suspects by the police.[4] Tape-recording of interviews became the norm as a result, but it took time to implement — time that resulted in a number of serious miscarriages of justice before tape-recording was introduced or available. However, it was later expanded to record contact with

---

3. *The Report of the Royal Commission on Criminal Procedure*, chaired by Sir Cyril Phillips (1978-81), London: HMSO.

4. *A Practical Approach to Criminal Procedure* (1982), John Sprack, Oxford: Oxford University Press. This analyses both the Commission itself and PACE. *Regulating Policing: The Police and Criminal Evidence Act 1984 Past, Present and Future* (2008), Ed Cape and Richard Young, Oxford: Hart Publishing, is another important text in this area.

significant witnesses as well, which is a welcome development that both protects witnesses from improper conduct and the police from spurious accusations of malpractice. Another important recommendation resulted in the cps being established.

The Royal Commission considered the Maxwell Confait Inquiry. The forensic pathology in that case had been a complete mess to put it mildly. Cameron, Teare and Simpson were certain regarding their findings, but they were all wrong and by a considerable distance. Each of them had assumed that rigor mortis was just setting in after the fire. In actual fact it was fading. Confait had been dead for two days before his body was discovered. Professors Keith Mant and Alan Usher confirmed this finding by the discolouration of organs—a far more reliable indicator of the phase of rigor mortis.

The fire at Doggett Road that had interested police so much in Lattimore, Leighton and Salih in the first place had nothing to do with Confait's murder at all. They were clearly innocent, but who was responsible for Confait's murder? Detective chief superintendent E George and inspector Edward Ellison identified two important suspects and interviewed them while they were in prison. Douglas Franklin confessed to the murder and Paul Pooley admitted being there when Confait was killed. Franklin committed suicide in 1980 soon after being interviewed by George. The confessions were accepted by the authorities, but Franklin's death prevented vindication by the conviction of the truly guilty. Nevertheless, the then Attorney General Sir Michael Havers declared Lattimore, Leighton and Salih innocent, vindicating them in all but name. The same occurred in Sean Hodgson's case,[5] which began while the Royal Commission was gathering evidence.

The three young men were compensated for their ordeal. Fisher was summoned by Lord Havers, Lord Chancellor, and invited to accept the findings, but refused to despite the evidence. He never retracted his plainly erroneous belief in spite of the evidence. The three had been represented at the successful appeal by Sir Louis Blom-Cooper qc, who criticised Fisher's conclusions, pointing out many flaws such as that Salih had not even been charged with Confait's murder, yet Fisher declared him guilty of it—a trick that had been used to deny Timothy Evans the vindication he deserved in

---

5. See mainly the *Introduction* and *Chapter 3*.

1966. The vindication of the Catford Three as they were known sounded the death knell of the old eras of policing and prosecutions too. Eventually the demand for change proved too loud to ignore, largely due to that case and the acceptance of their vindication. The modern era of criminal justice was about to begin, but the methods used to delay vindicating the Catford Three were tried and tested and had ultimately failed again.

Posthumous Relief

Confessions had been extracted wrongly from innocent people before the Catford Three. Timothy Evans was a vulnerable man induced to falsely confess to crimes committed by depraved serial killer John Christie. Evans was executed on March 9th 1950. Christie had been a crucial prosecution witness and was portrayed as a respectable man by prosecuting counsel, Travers Christmas Humphreys KC.[6] Humphreys was convinced of Evans' guilt and Evans stood no chance at his appeal — the appeal judges included the father of the prosecution's King's Counsel, Mr Justice (Sir Travers) Humphreys, who shared his son's belief that Evans was guilty of the murder of his baby daughter Geraldine. The notoriously pro-hanging Lord Chief Justice (Rayner) Goddard and Mr Justice (Sir Frederic) Sellers were the other judges. That left the then Home Secretary, James Chuter-Ede, as Evans' last hope of avoiding execution. A reprieve was not forthcoming and Albert Pierrepoint put Evans to death.

Three years later the "respectable witness" was exposed as the beast that he was, but the cover-up began early and at top level. The Attorney General, Sir Lionel Heald QC led the prosecution of Christie and allowed the police to say they had no concerns whatsoever that the wrong man had been hanged in 1950. Christie was duly convicted and did not appeal. It was patently obvious that whoever killed Geraldine had also killed Evans' wife Beryl. Despite confessing to both murders, Evans was never prosecuted for Beryl's murder — just Geraldine's, but despite also confessing to both crimes Christie

---

6. The then monarch's father, George VI, was King at the time. Top barristers were therefore known as King's Counsel if they had taken silk. As of February 1952 they became QCs.

was never charged with either murder. Christie had killed several women in the same fashion as Beryl and Geraldine. The odds of two separate killers who murdered in exactly the same fashion living at the same address at the same time were pretty low, to put it mildly, and Evans had accused Christie of killing Beryl and Geraldine at a time that he could not have known that Christie was a serial killer, let alone one whose method of killing was exactly the way that Geraldine and Beryl were murdered. The day would come when Christie would be unmasked as one of Britain's most notorious serial killers.

It was obvious that something had to be done, but Chuter-Ede's successor, Sir David Maxwell-Fyfe, was determined that there would be no public inquiry under any circumstances. The fallout from Christie's exposure and the likelihood that British justice had executed an innocent man would be kept under control on Maxwell-Fyfe's watch. Neither the CJS, nor politicians would own up quickly and relatively painlessly that a terrible miscarriage of justice had occurred, partly through incompetence in the original inquiry that resulted in Evans' conviction. Instead, the inquiry headed by John Scott-Henderson QC, left much to be desired, but that would not be the end of the story.[7]

Thirteen years after Christie was executed the fate of Timothy Evans had to be dealt with, but even then it was done grudgingly.[8] The report by Mr Justice (Sir Daniel) Brabin suggested that he had simply been hanged for the wrong crime—one he had not even been tried for. Then Home Secretary Roy Jenkins pardoned Evans, but the controversy continued until 2004. Evans' case eventually helped to abolish the death penalty for murder. The then Labour MP, Sydney Silverman, wrote persuasively about the case, which was also taken up by the journalist Harold Evans (no relation). Silverman's 1965

---

7.   *Hanged and Innocent* (1953), Reginald Paget QC and Sidney Silverman MP, London: Victor Gollancz.

8.   There are several publications on this case such as the lawyer Michael Eddowes' book *The Man on Your Conscience: An Investigation of the Evans Murder Trial,* Cassell and Co. Eddowes was the first to champion Evans' innocence and ironically his son, John, was one of the last to claim that Evans was guilty. The late Sir Ludovic Kennedy's *Ten Rillington Place,* Victor Gollancz , is the best known of those works campaigning to prove Evans' innocence after an official inquiry concluded that Evans was guilty of both murders. It was also referred to in Bob Woffinden's book, *Miscarriages of Justice,* Hodder and Stoughton. John Eddowes claimed in a 1995 book, *The Two Killers of Rillington Place,* that no miscarriage of justice had occurred, Warner Books. He has subsequently been proved wrong.

Bill suspended the death penalty for murder for five years with an option to make abolition permanent within that period, which happened in 1969. After Britain incorporated the European Convention on Human Rights into domestic law through the Human Rights Act, the death penalty was eventually abolished for all offences, but Evans' family had a long wait for the obvious to be fully acknowledged.

Nevertheless, Evans' case remains controversial. He was accused of a crime he had not been charged with — Beryl's murder. Convictions of deceased people have been overturned, but Evans' conviction was not. He was pardoned, but that did not satisfy his family. In March 2004 the Criminal Cases Review Commission refused to refer his case back to the Court of Appeal, claiming that "there would have been no advantage to be gained by [doing so]". It believed that the pardon granted in 1966 established that it was a miscarriage of justice and provided adequate remedy, including the restoration of his reputation to Evans.[9]

Evans' case was taken up by solicitor Bernard de Maid who represented his half-sister, Mary Westlake. After the CCRC refused to refer Evans' case back for appeal, his family decided to challenge that decision by judicial review. Nobody argued that it was anything other than a serious miscarriage of justice, but Mr Justice (Sir Andrew) Collins and Mr Justice (Sir Stanley) Burnton were not prepared to overturn the CCRC's decision as they did not believe that it was wrong. De Maid had previously described it as "outrageous". Instead of having the case referred back for an appeal, which the judges conceded he was bound to win, they declared Evans innocent of the murder of Geraldine Evans — the crime he was hanged for. They then addressed the Brabin fallacy.

"No jury could properly have convicted him of murdering his wife and he must be regarded as innocent of that charge too," Collins said when making the unprecedented declaration of innocence for a crime that Evans did not face trial over. Although Evans' conviction has never been quashed and Christie was never convicted of either crime, there is little doubt that Timothy Evans was innocent of the murders of both Geraldine and Beryl

---

9. Timothy Evans originally hailed from the Merthyr Vale in South Wales, although the miscarriage of justice leading to his execution occurred in and concerned events in London.

Evans and that Christie was responsible for these crimes. For these reasons Evans should be seen as vindicated as both his innocence and Christie's guilt have been officially acknowledged. Shamefully it took over half a century to achieve, but Evans' case played a huge part in the abolition of the death penalty, partly because he had been vindicated in the court of public opinion. The law took decades to catch up. The previous case of vindication never involved a risk of execution, but it was equally important and so is worth setting out in some detail — that of the alleged fraudster Adolph Beck.[10]

A Failure

For a decade Beck fought to make ends meet to keep his struggling mining venture afloat. He had made a few enemies as he talked people into investing in the failing business without clearing his debts. Beck had plenty of motive to steal, but instead he was the victim of misidentification twice. Despite his financial embarrassment, Beck was determined to keep up appearances as a pillar of the community — top hat, monocle and cane — but appearances were deceptive. He had left a trail of debts and angry people. Nevertheless, he was soon to become a victim of circumstance. In November 1895 a man who did not bear an "uncanny" resemblance to Beck (see later for the significance of these words) struck up a conversation with Ottilie Meissonier on the same street that Beck lived on and then accompanied her home. He relieved her of property worth £30 — a substantial amount in those days. She could not believe her eyes when in the evening of December 16th she saw a man she was convinced was the scoundrel. He smiled at her before she told him that she knew him. Beck's ordeal was about to begin in earnest. She accused him of theft and he panicked and ran — both ironically trying to get to the police.

Beck accused her in strong terms and she responded with the accusation of theft — a genuine one though aimed at the wrong person. He was arrested and they were both taken to a nearby police station, but Beck was not believed. The robbery of Meissonier matched details of a previous one

---

10. See *The Strange Case of Adolph Beck* (2001), Tim Coates, London: Stationery Office Books.

that happened to Daisy Grant a few months earlier. Grant's description of the villain matched Beck. Police had no doubt who was telling the truth.

Beck was put into an identification parade and seven men who had seen the swindler picked him out as did Meissonier's servant and Grant as well. Beck was remanded into custody protesting his innocence. The story made headline news, which encouraged other victims to come forward. Before long 12 victims had identified Beck as having swindled them, with varying degrees of certainty, and there were other witnesses too. The case against him looked cast iron.

The prosecution had a hand-writing expert, Thomas Gurrin, who claimed that examples of the swindler's writing kept by some victims was a disguised version of Beck's. The swindler's methods of selecting victims and committing his crimes fitted a pattern. Most of them had pretensions of respectability, or wealth without the means to back it up — some were supplementing their income through prostitution. The swindler was amiable and struck up conversations, claiming to be Earl Wilton, Lord Wilton or Lord Wilton de Willoughby; he would accompany the women to their homes offering them the position of housekeeper. He would pass cheques and ask to see their jewellery and offer to buy better quality things for them and clothes, but would take some of theirs in order to have their size or after promising to mount jewels better. The cheques were worthless and he kept these items.

Travesty

Both the police and Beck's solicitor knew of an important fact — the one thing that Beck had in his favour. Nearly 20 years earlier there had been a similar series of crimes. It was quite obvious that the current crime wave was the work of the same man. The 1877 crimes were committed by a man who called himself John Smith. He was prosecuted by Forrest Fulton, who was appointed the trial judge for Beck's case and would conduct it shamefully as Fulton knew that Beck was innocent. If the 1877 victims identified Beck, then he was guilty, but if not he was innocent. Beck desperately needed the 1877 crimes to be admissible as it was his only hope. He was unable to provide alibis for any of the crimes and he was wrongly believed to resemble the phoney peer Earl Wilton. However, Sir Forrest Fulton cut Beck's defence to shreds by forbidding any mention of the 1877 crimes.

Gurrin had said that both handwriting samples from the 1877 crimes and 1895 were written by the same man, but the prosecutor Horace Avory (later to become Mr Justice (Sir Horace) Avory, a notorious hanging judge), only questioned him about the latter ones to prevent the defence, which was presented by Charles Gill, who subsequently took silk, from playing his trump card. Gill's objections cut no ice with Fulton who insisted that previous convictions could not be used, so the 1877 material was ruled out.

Avory shrewdly would not allow police constable Elliss Spurrell to give evidence at the trial, even though he had testified at the committal hearing, because he had arrested Smith in 1877, which would have given Gill his opportunity to show that Beck was not Smith. Beck no longer stood a chance, but Spurrell was not the only veteran of the 1877 case. The judge himself could have been a defence witness that would have prevented a gross miscarriage of justice! Fulton later claimed that mention of the 1877 offences would have harmed the defence and that it was his responsibility to steer the trial correctly, to deal only with the crimes that the accused was charged with. Robbed of his only hope of proving innocence, Beck was convicted — on overwhelming identification evidence — every witness having made an honest and genuine mistake.

Beck was sentenced to five years hard labour. He continued to protest his innocence and actually proved it while in prison, but yet again it was shamefully ignored. John Smith was recorded as being a Protestant until his Jewish faith, which he proved by demonstrating that he had been circumcised, was acknowledged in his prison file in 1879. The Governor of Portland Prison examined Smith's file and observed this, so he examined Beck and found clear evidence that Beck was not Smith — the Norwegian had not been circumcised. There was no longer any doubt that Beck was innocent, but the authorities didn't care — there was no right of appeal then. The evidence was sent to Sir Forrest Fulton, but the judge refused to entertain it and it was "buried". The Home Office had absolute proof of Beck's innocence in 1898, but it made no difference whatsoever.

Even Beck was not told of it. Having served his five years he was freed in 1901, aged 60, only to have a repeat dose in 1904 when Pauline Scott went to police on March 23rd to complain that she had been swindled by Lord Willoughby. Beck was confronted with yet another woman identifying him as the swindler and more followed. Rose Reece, Caroline Singer and Grace Campbell also identified him. He stood trial again before Mr Justice (Sir William) Grantham and was convicted yet again, but ten days later the elusive John Smith struck again, swindling sisters Violet and Beulah Turner.

The method was identical and this time there was no doubt that Beck was innocent as he had the perfect alibi—he was in Brixton Prison! Ironically, this time Beck didn't need an alibi as the Turners had second thoughts and had the man followed. He went to a pawnbroker and the police came and arrested him. Several more victims of Smith surfaced and the swindler owned up to his crimes, which included the ones Beck had been convicted of. Smith was identified as Wilhelm Meyer, an Austrian-born surgeon who had fallen upon hard times and taken to crime. Finally, Beck's appalling luck changed. The truth emerged, including the circumcision evidence. He was freed and pardoned of both the 1895 and 1904 offences. An outraged public and media demanded that Beck be compensated properly. A £2,000 offer was dismissed on Beck's behalf by a disgusted media. Five thousand pounds was agreed, but Beck, by now a bitter and broken man, died in December 1909.

The Lessons

It was obvious that something had to be done about this. The Beck case is frequently cited concerning the dangers of identification evidence, but incredibly every single one of these mistaken identifications was genuine. The government was forced to react to the scandal. It ordered an inquiry headed by the then Master of the Rolls, Sir Richard Collins. There were two major failings of the system and both involved Sir Forrest Fulton. His decision to exclude the 1877 offences from the 1896 trial was wrong in law and deprived Beck of his right to a fair trial and the Home Office knew that Beck was not Smith in 1898 due to the circumcision evidence, which Sir Forrest also knew about, but both shamefully concealed the truth. The Home Office was roundly condemned over this, but Fulton was no better. His behaviour was nothing short of a conspiracy to pervert the course of justice and he should have faced trial over it. Instead, he remained as Recorder of London until he resigned due to ill-health in 1922. He died in June 1925, having outlived his victim by over 15 years.

The identification evidence was farcical too as beyond a superficial similarity of some features Beck and Smith were far from doubles. They looked nothing like each other, but 16 victims, each of whom had spent an hour in the company of the notorious swindler, had wrongly identified Beck as the man concerned. Without that evidence the case against Beck could not have proceeded.

The lasting legacy of the vindication of Beck was the establishing of the Court of Criminal Appeal in 1907. Clearly, vindication is not only a powerful force for change, it has been proved effective in the past and DNA-testing led it into the modern age.

CONCLUSION

Vindication of the Cardiff Five

THE CASE OF THE CARDIFF FIVE is unique for many reasons, but there is nothing unusual about the individual components of it. People confess to crimes they have not committed for many reasons. Some implicate other innocent people too. Retractions occur without being believed. Witnesses give false testimony. Forensic science is manipulated. Offender profilers lead police down the wrong track and arrests occur without sufficient evidence to justify them. There is nothing new in this, but tragic as the Cardiff Five case is, there are still lessons to learn beyond current events.

Many years ago I got involved in this case because I saw that although justice may miscarry all too frequently — it is perhaps inevitable in any justice system — that there was something especially troubling about it, even if it did not involve the risk of execution, the fate that befell Mahmood Mattan four decades before the Cardiff Five stood trial.

Mattan paid the ultimate price when in September 1952 he was hanged for a murder he did not commit. His young wife and family were left to deal with the stigma for almost half a century. The Welsh detective Harry Power claimed that justice had been done in his book despite serious flaws. His colleague Ludon Roberts had interviewed a Somalian man who fitted the description of the killer. Tehar Gass was a violent man — Mattan was not. Gass was sent to Broadmoor two years later for killing Granville Jenkins, but Mattan was defended poorly and rushed to the gallows. These methods were effective. "Criminals" were arrested and swiftly brought to justice. Society and the CJS were content. Why wouldn't they be? But the foundations were rotten. The innocent who denied and protested and fought for their lives had become indistinguishable from the guilty who falsely protested their innocence. The suffering of the innocent seemed a small price to pay for security, but this was false comfort.

Nobody is protected by the conviction of the innocent. The fictitious sixth sense was no substitute for credible evidence. Police officers were not the inheritors of Tiresias' mantle.[1] But it was effective. The CJS continued to rely on such evidence, even if it produced incredible cases and rotten convictions.

While convictions were secured and public confidence remained high why would they change? But the Lynette White Inquiry changed all of that. These methods — ones that had been so successful — turned to dust belatedly. The Cardiff Five were wholly innocent. There is no longer any doubt that Jeffrey Gafoor was the real murderer. Evidence proved it and he accepted his guilt. With the notable exception of South Wales Police, no professionals working within the CJS, or organizations charged with regulating the relevant professions, have taken responsibility for what happened or, to my knowledge, developed best practice as a result. The case is far from an isolated example, but it offers the best ever opportunity to learn the lessons of an extraordinarily tragic case. Remarkably the story and the lessons it offers still remain almost unknown nearly ten years on.

Despite several miscarriages of justice being resolved by proof of innocence through the unequivocal conviction of another person, identification where the true offender had died or comprehensive proof that no crime occurred, only one inquiry — that into the Lynette White case — was determined to learn the lessons of what went wrong. Why? The lessons of how this terrible crime was solved and its implications have yet to be taken on board. It is astonishing how little has been appreciated and understood when it remains a unique blueprint of what to do on so many levels. Vindication can change the CJS as a whole and deliver a just and efficient system.

Justice and Reconciliation

As described in earlier chapters, Jeffrey Gafoor allowed innocent men to go to prison for a total of 16 years for his crime. Their lives have been wrecked and those of their families. He has left a trail of devastation for Lynette White's family also. These families have had to cope with the guilt of believing the

---

1. The legendary Theban prophet who could see into the future in Ancient Greece.

Cardiff Five guilty, someone brandishing a gun at an innocent man—and much more besides. The care needs of the Cardiff Five, their families and Lynette's family have been ignored. While the Coalition government considered tariff reform, the needs of the innocent were ignored.

Knowingly allowing innocent people to have their lives wrecked in this way ought to be a criminal offence, or at the very least a defined aggravating circumstance when imposing sentence. Gafoor can express his remorse; he can apologise at will. He can address his offending behaviour. He can attend all the courses necessary and then some. He can progress effortlessly through the system to eventual release. The regime is devised to assist the guilty who can demonstrate that they are coming to terms with their crimes.

Meanwhile, those members of the Cardiff Five who were wrongly convicted and received life sentences could not progress in prison without causing further damage to themselves (i.e. by admitting to an offence that they had not committed). There is a real danger that Gafoor will serve less actual time in prison than they did as a whole—which graphically illustrates the need for change.

This book is not about revenge, it is about the future. It is essential that the wrongs of the past are addressed for justice to move on. The way the crime was solved is vitally important. Other miscarriages of justice can be resolved, prevented even through the methods used to resolve the Lynette White case. Incredibly, defendants, campaigners and lawyers remain unaware of the potent tool at their disposal. There has never been a more important weapon for justice than vindication, but to understand and appreciate its power, it is essential to understand how this miscarriage of justice happened and what resolving it has achieved and still could.

A Need for a Fully Independent Judicial Inquiry

Tony Paris' wait for an apology was not a long one. Sir Anthony Burden, chief constable of South Wales Police, apologised in writing for the failures of his force—he was not the chief constable when the Cardiff Five were given no choice but to stand trial. On July 7th, 2003, three days after Gafoor made history by becoming the first murderer in British history to resolve a miscarriage of justice by someone else pleading guilty, Burden wrote to the Cardiff Five and Lynette's family, not only apologising for the force's failures, but promising an investigation of what had gone wrong.

There had been numerous examples of the police investigating themselves without identifying what had happened in miscarriage of justice cases before. Why would this be different? For once, there was no doubt about innocence as the DNA evidence established Jeffrey Gafoor's guilt and the killer admitted that he had brutally murdered Lynette on his own. That again meant that the alleged eye-witnesses in the Cardiff Five case had perjured themselves. The question was not did they lie, but why did they lie?

Detective chief superintendent Chris Coutts was put in charge of this investigation. Over the years his team reduced. The investigators had powers of arrest and used them to secure evidence. They interviewed many people in their evidence-gathering process. I was one of them. Thirty-four people were subsequently arrested and interviewed under caution. Twenty of them were then either serving or retired police officers, who were investigated on suspicion of offences including conspiracy to pervert the course of justice and perjury. The highest ranking of them was the former head of South Wales Police CID, detective chief superintendent John Williams.

A forensic scientist, John Whiteside, was also interviewed under caution. The other 13 were civilian witnesses. It was a long drawn out process that involved lay advisers, the IPCC and the Special Crimes Division of the CPS, which, in 2007, decided to charge the four alleged eye-witnesses, Paul Atkins, Mark Grommek, Angela Psaila and Learnne Vilday with eleven counts of perjury between them — that covered their evidence at the committal hearing and the two trials. The charges excluded their statements. That decision denied them a defence of duress, even though, judge, jury, defence and prosecution all accepted that they had been bullied into making the incriminating statements in November and December 1988. Duress is no defence to perjury and that resulted in Grommek, Psaila and Vilday having no option but to plead guilty in October 2008 — Atkins was deemed medically unfit to stand trial.

The "New Cardiff Three", i.e. those witnesses in the original trial who were subsequently convicted of perjury, were jailed for 18 months each. Their trial judge, Mr Justice (Sir David) Maddison, had branded the conduct that they had been subjected to by the police as something that is "unacceptable in a civilised society." A few months later the CPS announced that 13 police officers would face trial for conspiracy to pervert the course of justice. Graham Mouncher would also face perjury charges as would the witnesses, Ian Massey and Violet Perriam.

Legal argument raged for over two years. The trials were severed due to the difficulties of having 15 defendants in the dock at the same time. Rachel O'Brien was found medically unfit to face trial. Originally eight officers and the two witnesses were to face the first trial that had been due to start in May 2011, but the health of John Bryan Gillard meant that he was dropped from this first batch. Swansea Crown Court—a stone's throw from The Guildhall, which had hosted the two trials of the Cardiff Five—was the venue. Mouncher, Thomas Page and Richard Powell were the highest ranking officers to face trial. They were joined in the dock by Michael Daniels, Peter Greenwood, Paul Jennings, John Seaford and Paul Stephen.

Depending on the outcome of that trial, John Murray, Stephen Hicks, Wayne Pugh and possibly Gillard might also face trial. Along with Massey and Perriam, the eight former officers pleaded not guilty.

The prosecution failed to complete its case. On December 1st, 2011 Nicholas Dean QC informed the court that copies of documents concerning an unrelated complaint to the IPCC by John Actie and three other files—also copies and seemingly irrelevant—could not be located. Coutts was accused of having ordered them to be shredded. That claim—an incorrect one as it turned out—was nonetheless accepted at face value and because the CPS decided that it could not give an undertaking that it had not happened with other documents, Dean "threw in the towel". Mr Justice (Sir Nigel) Sweeney recorded not guilty verdicts concerning all of the defendants. The possible "second trial" (mentioned above) was also stopped a week later on the same basis.

The biggest ever police corruption trial over a miscarriage of justice anywhere in the world had ended in a most unsatisfactory manner. Coutts was not given the opportunity to defend himself and to assert that he had not ordered the documents to be shredded. The whole situation seems a little absurd. The documents were copies and the complaint by Actie was not generated by the police—it came from the IPCC. The originals had been disclosed, but the copies had not been. Defence lawyers complained of non-disclosure (which given the extent of non-disclosure of far more pertinent material in the two trials of the Cardiff Five, seems ironic).

The disclosure officer—he had left the inquiry at the time of the 2011 trial—was detective sergeant Mark Allen. "Mr Allen was contacted and he confirmed that he did recollect at some point being asked to destroy some material, although the recollection was vague," Dean said. Allen made a statement confirming this "vague recollection". As Dean told the court:

> Early on 29th November detective sergeant [Eddie] May was able to consult his records of work he had done as office manager for the investigating team. He found an entry in his records for 24th February of 2010 recording his ongoing audit of material held by the investigation and a conversation with detective sergeant Allen in which detective sergeant Allen had confirmed that *he had destroyed the copies of the four files of* IPCC *material seemingly because in relation to one of the files Mr Coutts had instructed him to dispose of it and in relation to the remaining three because Mr [James] Haskell had said they were irrelevant.* In fact, six months or so earlier Mr Haskell had clearly indicated that they were relevant and potentially at least disclosable. [Italics supplied]

These were serious suggestions but Coutts was not asked or given the chance to explain. There was no adjournment to get a full explanation from him or Haskell but Dean did say that the explanation of the destruction of the documents was likely to be consistent with "serious error rather than deliberate misconduct". But what if they had not been destroyed at all? They were in fact found in January 2012, they had never been shredded and were still in the original box in which they had been sent to the force by the IPCC. Neither Dean nor the CPS appeared to even contemplate this possibility. Instead Dean consulted with Simon Clements, a senior member of the CPS, to decide where events left the prosecution.

"It was and is clear to us," Dean told the jury, "that the apparently deliberate destruction of documents would inevitably be fatal to this case." But there was a problem—as it would later emerge. In fact not only had the documents not been destroyed deliberately, they had not been destroyed at all! Dean continued by saying, "The decision to dispose of documents was itself deliberate … The decision, though, was not recorded in any way and it came to light by pure chance. The decision involved not only the senior investigating officer but also the officer who was at the time the lead disclosure officer." Again, Dean was mistaken in so far as any actual destruction had taken place, so the court was not getting a true picture. "The subject of some of the destroyed material was one of the original defendants, one of the men with whom the police are alleged to have had an inappropriately close relationship, and the material was, in fact, disclosable, if not primary disclosure, then certainly in secondary disclosure," Dean told the court.

Dean continued: "The fact that the material had been destroyed after primary disclosure meant that it could not have been re-reviewed in secondary disclosure, and this has to be set against assurances that I have repeatedly given that all material had, in fact, been re-reviewed for secondary disclosure purposes". But the material had not been destroyed and secondary disclosure could have occurred. "The fact that the material had been destroyed meant that it was impossible to say for certain whether the material retrieved from the IPCC on Monday was, in fact, exactly the same material that had been reviewed and then destroyed," he said. "That the decision to destroy the material was not recorded, particularly given to whom it related, meant that it would be impossible for me to give meaningful reassurance that no other material had been treated similarly and impossible to give meaningful reassurances that other potentially important instructions about the treatment of unused material had also not been recorded."

"Now the decision to at least separate but still retain some of the IPCC material would have been justifiable," Dean told the court. But what happened is that it was retained and had not been separated. The documents remained in the very boxes that they had been sent to South Wales Police in. Although investigations as to what happened are still taking place it appears to represent a failure of the system that these documents could not be properly accounted for.

"As it is, it seems likely detective sergeant Allen took what Mr Coutts said as an instruction to destroy more wide-ranging material, and in any event the decision was not, as I have repeatedly said, recorded, as it very clearly should have been," Dean told the court. "The appearance of this against the background of the other disclosure difficulties that my Lord has outlined and the allegations of impropriety made against Mr Coutts and the investigation more generally is, of course, irredeemable," he said.

"It has to be acknowledged that the appearance of what has occurred is itself very damaging indeed," Dean said. "For those reasons the prosecution can no longer sustain a position maintaining that the court and the defendants can have confidence in the disclosure process, the confidence that my Lord has referred to with all its importance to our criminal justice system."

It was to transpire that detective sergeant Allen's vague recollections were incorrect. He had not destroyed these documents, deliberately or otherwise, and if a reasonable time had been given to search for them the documents may well have been located, an officer's reputation would not have been questioned and an important trial might not have collapsed. In truth the missing documents had not been destroyed and whether or not Dean or the CPS should have taken further steps in relation to them and they did not know the true picture when the judge decided that the trial had to stop. But where does all this leave confidence in the criminal justice system?

"The developments in this case over the last few days and weeks have been discussed in detail with the Director of Public Prosecutions," Dean told the court. "He is deeply concerned about the decision he has had to now confirm and the reasons for it. He agrees that it is necessary that no further evidence be offered and that not guilty verdicts be directed." Quite why the CPS did not ask for time to search for or verify the position in relation to the documents remains a matter that will no doubt be looked into as part of ongoing inquiries.

"The director and the chief constable for South Wales Police wish me to make clear that they have already directed that there be a full and detailed review of all the circumstances in which this decision has had to be made," Dean said. "That is a review that will have the full support and cooperation of the South Wales Police. Contingent upon fact-finding, the review may involve a subsequent reference to the Independent Police Complaints Commission." Meanwhile South Wales Police did refer the case to the IPCC so that this will take place at the same time as that announced by the Director of Public Prosecutions, Keir Starmer QC, who made arrangements for an investigation as to why the prosecution failed and called in HM Crown Prosecution Service Inspectorate (HMCPSI).

Almost nine years ago Coutts and his team asked for patience and trust, insisting that they wanted to get to the truth of what had happened and the chance to put right what the force had got wrong. I believed then that they were sincere and still do. That investigative process should have been the blueprint for police and others anxious to reclaim ground and convince a sceptical public that it was possible to put matters right following a miscarriages of justice. Now, in my view, an independent judicial inquiry has never been needed more, into the workings of the criminal justice system as a whole. A process designed to demonstrate accountability and prove that this was unnecessary has ended by strengthening these demands.

The IPCC appointed Sarah Green, a commissioner from the Midlands to head its investigation and both the IPCC and DPP adapted their terms of reference after the rediscovery of the allegedly lost documents. Sarah Green explained:"The terms of reference for our independent investigation have been updated to reflect the discovery of the documents that the Lynette White trial was told had been destroyed ... This is a very tightly focused investigation that concentrates on events regarding the alleged destruction of IPCC documents that were referred to in Swansea Crown Court. We are not investigating the reasons for the collapse of the trial, which is a matter for the Director of Public Prosecutions".

Sarah Green promised to publish the IPCC's findings at the conclusion of the investigation. The terms of reference are as follows.

The IPCC investigation will seek:

1. To establish the date that each of the four specific copy files of documents came into the possession of the Disclosure Team on [Phase Three of] the Lynette White[2] investigation.

---

2. Coutt's investigation is known as the Lynette White Inquiry Phase Three or Operation Rubicon.

2. To establish what disclosure process each of the four specific copy files of documents was subjected to by any police officer or police staff member and any recording process used to detail that disclosure process.

3. To establish if any decision was made to destroy any of those four specific copy files of documents by any police officer or police staff member and if so whether any police officer or police staff member properly recorded the reasoning and rationale for such a decision.

4. To establish the movements and location of the four specific copy files of documents from the time they originally came into the possession of the Lynette White [Phase Three] investigation until their discovery on 17 January 2012 still in the possession of South Wales Police.

So far as the DPP is concerned, he announced that: "Shortly after the collapse of this trial I initiated a full and detailed review of the circumstances in which the decision to offer no further evidence was made … I asked leading counsel for the prosecution to prepare a comprehensive analysis of the reasons for the decision. I have now considered that analysis and as part of the review have decided to ask Her Majesty's Crown Prosecution Service Inspectorate, an independent statutory body, to consider the way in which the prosecution team conducted the disclosure exercise in this case." The amended terms of reference are as follows.

- Whether the prosecution team (CPS and counsel) approached, prepared and managed disclosure in this case effectively, bearing in mind the history, size and complexity of the investigation and prosecution;

- Whether the prosecution team (CPS and counsel) complied with their disclosure duties properly, including all relevant guidance and policy relating to disclosure, in light of the extensive material generated in this case;

- Whether the existing legal guidance is appropriate for cases of similar size and complexity;

- To make such recommendations as it feels appropriate in light of the examination and findings set out above, including, if appropriate, recommendations about CPS policy and guidance, and/or systems and processes, and CPS arrangements for the handling of cases of similar size and complexity.

Throughout all of this there is no mention of the original trials of the Cardiff Five nor of the fact that they, their families and Lynette White are the true victims of a continuing failure to get to the bottom of things. Even now, there is no definitive official account of all that has happened in one of Britain's most notorious miscarriages of justice. As a result, lessons remain unlearned and it seems the CJS as a whole is incapable of putting matters right, which leaves confidence dented.

It is now 24 years and counting since Lynette White was brutally killed and it is becoming ever more clear that only an independent judicial inquiry or possibly even a truth and justice commission-style investigation into the whole chain of events in this extraordinary case can establish what went wrong and provide the opportunity to prevent similar miscarriages of justice in future — and the time has long passed when justice should be delivered to all of those who became victims of this case.

And What of the Collapsed Trial?

One of the ways in which we may have learned something about how mistakes came to be made in this case was the corruption trial which ended so abruptly in December 2011, leaving many people with a sense of unease. As already explained that trial was ended by the judge on the basis of a false belief — that copies of documents had been destroyed when they had not. In these highly unusual circumstances, I find it hard to believe that the Crown Prosecution Service is not seeking to persuade the Court of Appeal that the charges should be reinstated on the basis of that mistake. There can be no finality or closure until this issue is confronted: where demonstrably wrong assurances are given to a court so that there is never a real trial at all it is hardly a case of double jeopardy — not in my book.

Vindication

One-hundred-and-eighty-years ago the Merthyr Rising was a landmark moment in the struggles of the British working class, especially in Wales.[1] Protesting against cuts in wages and unemployment, it forced the Whig government to take notice. They sacked the debtors courts, returning debts and goods to their original owners. The army and some of the Argyll and Sutherland Highlanders were sent to Merthyr to restore order, firing on a crowd when they refused to disperse, killing some protesters. Enraged, the protesters took control of the whole town and it took the government several days to regain control. Reforms eventually followed, but the sacrifices of the Merthyr activists should never be forgotten. Twenty-three stood trial for various offences. Two were sentenced to death.

Lewis Lewis (Lewsyn yr Heliwr) was as close to an organizer as could be found. The seizure of his property helped spark the rising. It was returned to him. He was sentenced to death for robbery, but reprieved when a police officer insisted that Lewis had shielded him from harm. His 23-year-old nephew, Richard Lewis (better known as Dic Penderyn) was less fortunate. Despite a petition signed by 11,000 people, the Home Secretary, Lord Melbourne, was determined that at least one person was going to hang. Penderyn participated in the Merthyr Rising believing in a just cause. It cost him his life for a crime he did not commit.

---

1. Eight years after the Merthyr Rising, Newport rebelled in the Chartist cause. Several Chartists were killed or wounded and 200 were prosecuted in the aftermath of crushing the Newport Rising. Three were sentenced to be hung drawn and quartered, but following the intervention of the Lord Chief Justice, John Frost, Zephaniah Williams and William Jones had their sentences commuted to transportation for life. Frost was later celebrated in Newport, returning in triumph in 1856 after receiving an unconditional pardon. Eventually Chartism withered away, but its demands found favour and influenced movements worldwide. In the same year as the Newport Rising, another protest movement emerged in South Wales. The Rebecca Riots began as a protest against taxation and the collapse of prices for agricultural produce. The Merthyr Rising was the first in a tradition of working-class resistance and Richard Lewis is arguably its first martyr, certainly the first to be vindicated.

On June 3rd, 1831 a soldier with the 93rd Highland Regiment, Donald Black, was stabbed in the leg. This did not kill him and even his evidence suggested that Penderyn was innocent. Black never identified Penderyn as his attacker. The methods used to railroad Penderyn to the gallows were strikingly similar to other miscarriages of justice that occurred in South Wales decades later. James Abbott gave perjured testimony against Lewis. Without this, Penderyn could not have been convicted, let alone hanged.

Penderyn was hanged in Cardiff Market on August 13th, 1831. He protested his innocence to the last and had considerable support, but Melbourne,[2] wanted to deter others. Penderyn died a slow and agonising death, strangled by the noose—this happened decades before the long drop was pioneered by doctors in Ireland in the 1850s and used there. It was adopted by executioner William Marwood in 1872 and eventually became the favoured method of execution in Britain from 1875, which is significant in Penderyn's story.

With Penderyn dead, Abbott found a conscience and admitted perjuring himself, claiming that he did so on Melbourne's orders. There is little doubt that Penderyn was innocent.

Two years after Marwood hanged Frederick Horry at Lincoln Prison—the first time the length of the drop had been calculated to ensure the prisoner's neck was broken rapidly and that he or she died quickly—one participant in the Merthyr Rising lay dying. Ianto Parker confessed to the Congregational minister, the Reverend Evan Evans, that he, and not Penderyn, had stabbed Black in the leg. Black survived easily, but the offence was absurdly described as attempted murder and carried the death penalty at the time, so Parker, fearing either execution or, if lucky, transportation, fled the country, leaving Penderyn to hang. Despite the deathbed confession, Penderyn's case was not re-opened.

Deathbed confessions or statements of a dying man have been accepted as evidence for many years. In the nineteenth century religion played a greater role in people's lives—fear for their souls influenced them more than now.

---

2. William Lamb, became the second Viscount Melbourne in 1828. He was a Whig (the precursors of the Liberal Party) politician, who had a reputation as a reformer, yet some of his policies and practices refute this. He dealt with the Swing Riots of 1830-31 in a vastly different fashion to the Merthyr Rising. In Wales, an example was needed and Penderyn would do. Melbourne went on to become Prime Minister, the favourite of the young Queen Victoria. He died before Ianto Parker's death-bed confession proved Penderyn to be innocent.

It was therefore accepted by the law that a person on the brink of death had no reason to lie and every cause to clear his or her conscience, as they would soon be judged by God. Consequently such evidence was powerful. There is no reason to doubt Ianto Parker's sincerity or that of the Reverend Evan Evans under these circumstances. This all occurred before there was a Court of Criminal Appeal[3] and at a time when pardons were few and far between.

The mechanisms to quash Penderyn's conviction did not exist then, but do now. He remains convicted of a crime that he did not commit. If this conviction was referred back to the Court of Criminal Appeal based on the evidence that is now available—shamefully for nearly 140 years—it is hard to see how the conviction could be sustained. It is often said that there is no statute of limitations in Britain, yet Penderyn's case tells a different story. The crucial witness, without whom there was no credible case, admitted perjuring himself, after the execution. The victim did not identify Penderyn. The real perpetrator admitted his guilt on his death bed and the Reverend Evan Evans campaigned for justice after hearing that confession. The Criminal Cases Review Commission cannot possibly say that on the facts of this case there is not a real possibility that the conviction would be quashed if referred back for appeal. However the courts insist that an applicant who has been directly affected by the injustice must bring the case and this happened too long ago to affect their lives today, but why should that matter in the slightest. As Parris Glendenning said 82 years after the wrongful execution of John Snowden, "The search for justice has no statute of limitations. When faced with the possible miscarriage of justice, even from the distant past, our values compel us to take a second look". It would appear that there is no statute of limitations on the search for justice in Maryland, but there is in Britain. It should be quashed without delay. There was a long wait for Wales' second vindication case—almost 130 years, but half a century before the Cardiff Five were proved to be innocent another disgraceful miscarriage of justice rocked Butetown.

The last person to be hanged in Cardiff died on September 3rd 1952 at the hands of Albert Pierrepoint, but the most famous of Britain's executioners makes no reference to this in his memoirs.

---

3. And nowadays the Court of Appeal (Criminal Division).

A Major Hitch

Mahmood Mattan's name should never be forgotten. The young Somali seaman and father of three young children was completely innocent of the vicious murder of Lily Volpert. Evidence suppressed at his trial proves beyond doubt that not only was Mattan innocent, but also that the police had a good idea who the real killer was.

Tehar Gass was a dangerous man who went on to kill again, but did not face the gallows for either crime. Instead, the police and the CJS rushed an innocent man to the rope and resisted efforts to right that wrong for 46 years.

Mrs Volpert ran a shop in Bute Street, Butetown. She also functioned as a pawnbroker. On March 6th, 1952 her throat was slit. A weak circumstantial case was built up against Mattan, but the police knew well that, while Mattan was of Somali origin, he did not fit the description of a Somalian man leaving the scene of the crime at the relevant time given by the crucial witness, Jamaican carpenter, Harold Cover.

Cover was an unreliable witness at best, but was also suspected of the murder because of his violent tendencies. Mattan was hanged without knowing that before he was arrested, detective inspector Ludon Roberts had interviewed Gass, who fitted Cover's description to a tee. The man had a gold tooth—Mattan did not. There were other discrepancies too.

Mattan naïvely believed that British justice could not convict him because he was innocent. He plainly did not understand the court proceedings due to language difficulties, telling the authorities that they could give him a lawyer if they wanted to, but he wouldn't ask for one. In a trial dripping with racism, including from his defence counsel, T Rhys-Roberts, Mattan did not stand a chance. By today's standards that trial was a travesty—it also left much to be desired even in the 1950s. Rhys-Roberts undermined aspects of the prosecution case ably, but also invited the jury not to believe his client but rely on prosecution witnesses. His aim was to highlight discrepancies in the case using the prosecution witnesses, but the jury must have taken a dim view of anything Mattan said after that. If Mattan's lawyer was telling them not to believe him, they could surely dismiss everything that he had said, but Mattan's claims of innocence were absolutely true. Rhys-Roberts also described his client as "a semi-civilised savage" and "a half-child of nature". The late Lord Justice (Sir Frederick) Lawton said that he would have reprimanded any barrister who told a jury not to believe their client and who had described them in racist terms, but there were no reprimands for Rhys-Roberts.

Mattan's command of English was far from satisfactory to give instructions to his lawyer, let alone to give evidence, but he didn't ask for an interpreter. Despite his obvious language difficulties, Mr Justice (Sir Benjamin) Ormerod did not ensure that an interpreter was provided so a man on trial for his life understood the proceedings and could give evidence clearly. If he were the judge and it became clear that a witness or defendant did not understand the proceedings, Lawton would have stopped the proceedings until an interpreter was provided. He was incredulous that this had not happened. Even in the 1950s he found it hard to believe that so much had been allowed to go wrong.

The trial lasted just three days and the jury took slightly more than an hour and a half to find Mattan guilty. As the law then required, Ormerod sentenced him to death — there could be no recommendation for mercy, but Mattan still perversely believed that his innocence would protect him. It was a disgrace to every concept of justice that such a trial was allowed to occur, let alone result in a conviction, especially following such a flawed investigation, but he had the right of appeal, which would correct this travesty if British justice was truly as great as it claimed to be.

A month after Mattan was wrongly convicted, the Court of Criminal Appeal failed to correct matters. Mr Justice (Sir Patrick) Devlin, Mr Justice (Sir William) Gorman and Mr Justice (Sir Roland) Oliver rejected all of Rhys-Roberts' complaints about Ormerod's summing-up and refused to allow him to call fresh evidence to prove that the verdict was indeed perverse. Unsurprisingly, the racism of defence counsel and his undermining of his client and failure to ensure that Mattan understood the proceedings did not feature in the appeal. Rhys-Roberts was hardly likely to criticise his own conduct.

The police had concealed their knowledge of Gass and the effect that had on Cover's credibility from the judges. They had effectively ambushed the cjs and ensured that Mahmood Mattan would be judicially murdered, but instead of being criticised for concealing vital evidence, they were praised for "one of the finest collections of circumstantial evidence ever presented to the court", according to detective chief inspector Harry Power's autobiography. Crown counsel, Edmund Davies QC, was not even required to respond to Rhys-Roberts' arguments. The appeal was dismissed on August 19th, 1952.

The then Home Secretary, Sir David Maxwell-Fyfe,[4] declined to reprieve Mattan. Right to the bitter end Mattan believed that not only would he not be hanged, but that he would be freed as an innocent man. Nevertheless, the 28-year-old Somalian seaman was hanged for a crime he did not commit.[5] At least some City of Cardiff police officers — that force was later incorporated into South Wales Police — must have had an inkling that not only was Mattan innocent, but that they had almost certainly allowed the real killer to slip through their fingers and kill again. They showed no remorse for the judicial murder of Mahmood Mattan. Instead, the character assassination of an innocent man who could no longer defend himself continued. DCI Power was convinced that no miscarriage of justice had occurred and pointed out that the appeal court judges had praised the police on the quality of the circumstantial evidence that they had gathered. DCI Power also claimed that Mattan never forgot how they ritually slaughtered animals in his native Somalia. The killer had pulled Mrs Volpert's hair back to expose her throat, which he then slit. Presumably, every killer who uses such methods must also be familiar with the methods used to ritually slaughter animals in Somalia. DCI Power went to his grave, the police stayed silent and to the shame of his force never broke that silence. The truth was discovered through the efforts of Yusef Abdullahi's solicitor, Bernard de Maid, who took up Mattan's case to great effect in the 1990s, but what about Gass?

Gass was a sailor who quickly came to police attention due to his criminal activities. He was arrested, but allowed to leave, even though he had no alibi worthy of the name and had placed himself in the vicinity at the relevant time. He also had a liking for violence and went on to murder wages clerk Granville Jenkins, but was found not guilty by reason of insanity in 1954. Gass was detained in Broadmoor before being deported to British Somaliland,

4. Maxwell-Fyfe controversially refused to reprieve Derek Bentley — the feeble-minded teenager who was old enough to be executed for the murder of PC Sidney Miles, while his underage accomplice Christopher Craig was not. Even the trial judge, Lord Chief Justice Goddard, believed that Bentley should have been reprieved, despite a reputation as a hanging judge.
5. According to his family, he added four years to his age to allow himself to become a sailor.

as Somalia then was. Roberts knew that Gass fitted the description given by Cover, but withheld that information—and the fact that Gass placed himself at the scene of the crime at the relevant time—from the defence and the court. Gass was not heard of again. Had Ormerod, Devlin, Gorman and Oliver known about the police's knowledge of Gass and that it destroyed Cover's credibility, they would surely have prevented Mattan's conviction and execution and condemned the investigative methods that secured them, but the police ambushed the courts.

Meanwhile, Cover was also a man of appalling character. In 1969 he was convicted of the attempted murder of one of his daughters. He slit her throat with a razor, which was the same method used to kill Lily Volpert. It also emerged that he had been paid a reward for his evidence—testimony that prosecuting counsel John Williams QC accepted could not be relied on at all—during Mattan's appeal in 1998.

Forty-six years after Mattan was hanged, the Court of Appeal, headed by its then vice-president, Lord Justice (Sir Christopher) Rose, quashed Mattan's conviction. It was the first time that the conviction of a wrongly executed person had been quashed. Rose apologised for what had happened and the time it had taken to acknowledge—it could not be put right.

Mattan's family was compensated but, despite the size of the award, it proved insufficient as money could not replace a father of three young children, or remove the stigma that the family had wrongly endured for half a century. His widow Laura is now deceased and eldest son Omar drowned in mysterious circumstances.

This was also a case that laid bare shamefully racist attitudes. Mattan was not allowed to live in the same house as his wife, who was called "a black man's whore" by neighbours and the court proceedings were racist too. His children were treated as pariahs and were cruelly told about how their father died. Omar was eight-years-old when he learned the truth. He heard the Salvation Army Band playing and went out to sing with them. He was told that they didn't need the son of a hanged man.

Mattan's case and the treatment of his family disgraces Cardiff and its broader reputation for tolerance. It remains a sombre reminder of the consequences, not only of the death penalty preventing "mistakes" being rectified, but of the way that British justice functioned in those days.

The methods used to secure these scandalous convictions appear to have been passed down the ranks, resulting in other miscarriages of justice after capital punishment was abolished. But Richard Lewis and Mahmood Mattan are graphic reminders of when miscarriages had even worse consequences than those suffered by the Cardiff Five, Newsagents Three, Guildford Four and countless others. Those old miscarriages cannot really be rectified, ever.

Wales' longest-lasting miscarriage of justice ended as the last millennium came to a close. The Newsagents Three had lost eleven years each. One of its victims, Michael O'Brien, noticed that several cases involved a pattern of investigative methods reminiscent of the case of Richard Lewis (see *Appendix 1*) onwards. Confessions tended to be obtained from vulnerable suspects and these included accusations against other people too. Pressure was put on witnesses, especially vulnerable ones, outside the protection of the Police and Criminal Evidence Act 1984 (PACE). But there was more.

There were numerous abuses of PACE during this investigation that began in 1987. Perjury is a double-edged sword. It boxes witnesses in to a story that, once given, leads to fear of prosecution and makes retraction unlikely, especially after recent events. Prisoner informers, verbals, an absence of scientific evidence in extraordinary circumstances, or manipulation of it also played a part in a pattern of investigations that had been found wanting, eventually.

Stephen Miller's interviews had been tape-recorded but that did not protect him. According to the then Lord Chief Justice, Lord Taylor of Gosforth, Miller had been bullied and hectored, shouted down until he said what his interrogators wanted to hear. The requirements of PACE to record contact with Miller were observed in the Lynette White case and allowed Miller's taped interviews to be reviewed and ultimately corrected on appeal, but the abuses had been there all along, so it was no great triumph to have discovered these errors later.

The Newsagents Three were not so fortunate. Darren Hall was vulnerable too, but his interviews were not tape-recorded. Abuses of PACE were legion, but Hall took nine years to fight back. It needed a through examination to find the evidence that had been there from the beginning, but was either hidden or ignored for a decade, but once this started in earnest a pattern emerged.

Stuart Lewis appears to have been notorious for overhearing allegedly incriminating admissions in the cells area and other questionable practices. His evidence against O'Brien and Ellis Sherwood was one of the most important pieces of evidence against them. A persistent campaign for justice, led by O'Brien finally bore fruit. He wanted a public inquiry, Lewis brought to justice and an investigation of the methods used to convict him. In 2010, the Independent Police Complaints Commission (IPCC) agreed that it would supervise the investigation of Lewis, which meant that the policing issues, and there were several, would be looked into. There had been investigations conducted by the police into this case previously. Detective superintendent Chris Hobley of Norfolk Police was the senior investigating officer and had the opportunity to regain public trust with a thorough investigation. He was appointed in 2011, but Hobley retired without completing the job. He was replaced by detective superintendent Nicola Holland of Merseyside Police. Two witnesses who had admitted perjuring themselves in a television documentary and to the CCRC, Christopher Chick and Helen Morris, were arrested during the investigation, but in September 2011 the CPS decided that there was not sufficient evidence to prosecute them.

In the early 1980s, a Welsh Nationalist group that favoured armed struggle targeted property owned by absentee English landlords for bombing. Some nationalists were later arrested and stood trial in 1983, but they included people who were not involved in the bombing campaign. Daffyd Ladd pleaded guilty, but David Burns, Robert Griffiths, Nicholas Hodges and Adrian Stone were acquitted at trial. Gareth Westacott absconded, but subsequently returned to face trial and was also acquitted.

These acquittals were a setback for South Wales Police and especially Lewis as it clearly meant that his claim that Griffiths confessed to him was not being believed. Gerard Elias QC, who defended Tony Paris, prosecuted both the Explosives Conspiracy Trial and the Newsagents Three. He was the junior to the late Lord Williams of Mostyn in the earlier case.[1] During the Newsagents Three's appeal in 1999, Elias accepted that there had been "monkey-business" in relation to the Explosives Conspiracy Trial,[2] but there were other issues arising out of that case too.

Graham Mouncher was accused of serious malpractice by Hodges, who claimed that Mouncher's task was to bully and intimidate him and prevent him from getting rest. Hodges claimed that he was softened up by Mouncher

---

1. Gareth Williams went on to be chair of the Bar Council, a Home Office Minister and Attorney General in the final Labour government before the present Coalition.
2. For further information see *Police Conspiracy* (1984), John Osmond, Talybont: Y Lolfa.

and subsequently confessed to crimes he did not commit. This was before the era of PACE, let alone tape-recording of interviews, but the methods were similar and frightening. Hodges not only confessed, but implicated other people who he knew to be innocent. He was not suggestible like Miller or compliant like Hall and he certainly did not have a low intelligence quotient (IQ). Hodges went on to rise through the ranks of the Welsh Nationalist political party Plaid Cymru, becoming a councillor and serving as mayor. If a person like Hodges can be induced and intimidated into confessing to crimes that he did not commit without suffering from significant vulnerabilities, witnesses and suspects less equipped than he is are clearly vulnerable. It also showed how effective these methods can be.

Lewis was not involved in the Lynette White Inquiry, yet he loomed large in the controversy over the methods used by the force in several cases, especially as PACE was coming into force. There were too many for these methods to be coincidence and it could not be ignored indefinitely. Lewis and his methods were pivotal in the Newsagents Three's case and the Explosives Conspiracy Trial. Gerard Elias defended the late Paul Darvell. Along with his brother Wayne, Paul was wrongly convicted of the June 1985 murder of sex-shop manageress, Sandra Phillips. Don Carsley was the head of that inquiry during which vitally important evidence that could have identified and convicted the real killer was destroyed. They never got to the bottom of who gave the order for this to happen, even though it was a far more important destruction of evidence than that of the mere copies of documents that caused the collapse of the 2011 trial at Swansea Crown Court.

The Sandra Phillips Inquiry began a year before PACE became operational in 1986 and took seven years. South Wales Police claimed to have followed its requirements scrupulously. The judge and jury were assured that the interviews had been contemporaneously recorded and did not involve leading questions. Neither claim was true. Electrostatic depression analysis (ESDA) revealed previous versions that included telling the highly suggestible Wayne what they wanted to hear. An ear-ring that might have belonged to Phillips was "discovered" in a police car that had been used to bring Wayne Darvell to the police station for questioning, but that was not on the same day that Wayne had been in the car and after it had been searched previously. There were other irregularities as well, but the worst failing in this inquiry was the destruction of a blood-stained palm-print and the negatives of it as well. Once it was discovered that it did not match either of the Darvell brothers, work on it stopped and it was then destroyed. That was disgraceful. It also destroyed the possibility of it tying the real murderer to his crime.

The Darvell brothers were freed on appeal in 1992 after a previous application for leave to appeal had been dismissed. In 1992, the appeal judges, headed by Lord Taylor were horrified by what they had heard and their judgement reflected that. DCI Alun Thomas was the former head of Swansea CID. Along with detective inspector Jeffrey Jones and detective constable Michael Collins, Thomas stood trial for conspiracy to pervert the course of justice, at Chester Crown Court in 1994—they were acquitted. Carsley was never charged and it has never been explained who took the decision to destroy the blood-stained palm-print and the negative of it. That remains an inexplicable decision that hindered the later review of the case and may have protected the real killer from ever being brought to justice.

Later that year, the Cardiff Three won their appeal, but months later Jonathan Jones was arrested. It took the best part of three years for him to be freed on appeal in April 1996. His case bucked the trend, although there were some elements, such as the manipulation of scientific evidence, but another aspect was clearer. This was an inappropriate prosecution and suggested that the CPS was not doing its job as it should.

Another began as this was ending. Karen Skipper was walking her dogs by the River Ely. She was attacked in a manner that the judge thought bordered on the sadistic, undressed from the waist down, but not raped or sexually assaulted. Her hands were tied behind her back with her dogs' leads. She was thrown into the River Ely to drown by a particularly callous killer. Her estranged husband Phillip was questioned immediately and released, but five weeks later he was charged with her murder. This was also a case that South Wales Police were not convinced should have gone to trial. Skipper was acquitted in 1997, but subsequently died in November 2004 without seeing John Pope, who had featured in the original investigation, convicted of Karen Skipper's murder in February 2009.[3]

---

3. In 2010, Lord Justice (Sir John) Thomas, sitting with Mr Justice (Sir Nigel) Sweeney and Mrs Justice (Dame Nicola) Davies, quashed Pope's conviction and ordered a retrial.

At the same time another inappropriate prosecution had occurred, but this resulted in convictions. A fire on the Gurnos Estate in Merthyr Tydfil cost Diane Jones and her young children Shauna and Sarah-Jane their lives. Months later the case was "cracked" when under-age single-mother Carly John, who had initially supported Clarke's alibi, changed her story. She was arrested and interviewed under caution, suspected of conspiracy to pervert the course of justice.

John subsequently retracted her support of Clarke's alibi and became the crucial prosecution witness. As she was no longer a suspect the safeguards of PACE no longer applied. Clarke could not have John's interviews reviewed, or her examined for signs of vulnerability. This drove a coach and horses through the spirit of PACE, but there was a potentially vulnerable suspect too.

Denise Sullivan was originally listed as an alibi witness for Clarke too, but she retracted. Unlike John, Sullivan retracted again and was subsequently charged and convicted of conspiracy to pervert the course of justice. Clarke couldn't insist on Sullivan being checked for suggestibility or compliance either. Clarke and Hewins still wait to understand exactly what happened in those interviews. The recordings alone cannot demonstrate what they were thinking and why. Both John and Sullivan have yet to comply, so Clarke has no option but to wait and hope. This makes the dispensation of justice a lottery. Clarke and Hewins were found guilty of arson with intent to endanger life in 1997, although both were acquitted of manslaughter. The verdicts were bizarre as arson with intent to endanger life was much the same as manslaughter, but there were serious problems with the case against the women, especially Hewins. Prosecutor John Charles Rees QC's cross-examination of Hewins breached the rules on hearsay evidence. Hewins' conviction was quashed on that basis and a retrial was ordered in Clarke's case. The charges against her were allowed to "lie on the file".

It would later emerge that the police did not want to charge Hewins, but Rees[4] thought that she should be, which is important as the Crown

---

4. Rees defended John Actie at the second trial, Jonathan Jones throughout legal proceedings and was involved in the defence of the Newsagents Three at trial as well as prosecuting the Gurnos arson case. He also defended Jeffrey Gafoor and Geraldine Palk's killer, Mark Hampson, drawing criticism from the judge Mrs Justice (Heather, now Lady Justice) Hallett for the tactic of putting the victim's character on trial.

(prosecution lawyers) cannot be sued, although experts recently lost that privilege. Despite her conviction being unsafe, she has not received any compensation as the assessor, Baron Daniel Brennan QC, decided that she was not eligible. Another aspect of that case raising cause for concern was the manipulation of the scientific evidence regarding the components of petrol. The pattern appears to have applied to far more than just policing—the whole CJS in South Wales had failed repeatedly.

SOME FREQUENT ABBREVIATIONS

ACC—assistant chief constable
ACPO—Association of Chief Police Officers
BIA—behavioural investigative adviser
CCRC—Criminal Cases Review Commission
CCTV—closed circuit television
CID—Criminal Investigation Department
CJA—Criminal Justice Act (usually 2003)
CJS—Criminal Justice System
CODIS—Combined DNA Index System
CPS—Crown Prosecution Service
DC—detective constable
DCI—detective chief inspector
DCS—detective chief superintendent
DI—detective inspector
DNA—deoxyribonucleic acid
DPP—Director of Public Prosecutions
ECHR—European Convention on Human Rights
ECtHR—European Court of Human Rights
ESDA—electrostatic depression analysis
FBI—Federal Bureau of Investigation
FSS—Forensic Science Service
Interpol—International Criminal Police Organization
IPCC—Independent Police Complaints Commission
IQ—intelligence quotient
KC—King's Counsel
LAG—Lay Advisory Group
MP—Member of Parliament
MCRU—Major Crimes Review Unit
NCOF—National Crime and Operations Faculty
NIB—National Injuries Database
NPIA—National Policing Improvement Agency
PACE—Police and Criminal Evidence Act 1984

PC—police constable
QC—Queen's Counsel
SCAS—Serious Crime Analysis Section
SGM—second generation multiplex
SGM+—second generation multiplex plus
STR—short-tandem-repeats
UK—United Kingdom

INDEX

A

Abdullahi, Yusef *30, 37, 87, 98, 100, 104, 125*

accountability *xvi, 120, 121, 133*

accreditation *121, 133*

accusation

  unjust accusation *38*

ACPO *67*

  Homicide Working Group *68*

acquittal *38*

Actie, John *30, 31, 37, 87, 103, 104, 123, 125, 173*

Actie, Ronnie *30, 31, 87, 98, 125*

admission *99*

  cell admissions *189*

aggravation *36, 137, 139*

alcohol *117, 118*

alibi *42, 193*

Allen, Mike *174*

Anderson, Anthony *137*

anger *117, 118*

anonymous tip off *125*

apology *59, 89, 109, 110, 125, 127*

Applied Biosystems *52*

appropriate adult *156*

arson *193*

Ashworth, Dawn *48*

Association of Chief Police Officers (ACPO) *64, 133*

Atkins, Paul *172*

Attorney General *161*

B

Bain, Angus *155*

Barclay, Dave *33, 34, 67, 69, 77, 81, 84, 132*

Barratt, Tony *123*

Beck, Adolph *164*

behaviour

  behavioural analysis *45, 77, 81*

  behavioural investigative advice *133, 134*

  behavioural science *134*

  impulsive behaviour *117, 119*

Bethell, Paul *61, 94*

Birmingham Six *xiii, xx, 82*

Bishop, Marilyn *87*

Bissett, Samantha and Jazmine *114, 149*

Black Panther *52*

Blom-Cooper, Sir Louis QC *160*

blood *45*

  blood distribution patterns *49*

  blood group *45, 46, 75, 120*

  blood lust *130*

  blood-stains *46, 77, 83, 85*

  foreign blood *46, 85*

boiling oil/water *124*

Brabin, Mr Justice *162*

Brennan, Baron Daniel QC *194*

Bridge, Lord Justice *157*

Bridgend *105, 128*

Brinkmann, Bernd *51, 83*

British Psychological Society *115*
Britton, Paul *113, 121*
Broadmoor *114, 149, 186*
broken home *119*
brutality *37, 45, 97, 128, 139*
Buckland, Richard *48*
bullying *xiv, 172, 189*
  bullying admissions *156*
bungling *xvi*
Burden, Sir Anthony *64, 74, 110, 171*
Burnton, Mr Justice *163*
Butetown *37, 70, 76, 108, 118, 119, 124,*
    127, 184

C

Cameron, Professor James *155*
campaigners *43*
Campbell, Betty *70*
canteen culture *xiv*
Canter, David *116, 123*
Canton Police Station *40*
capital punishment *107*
cardboard box *84*
Cardiff *xx, 39, 46, 63, 70*
  Cardiff Crown Court *104*
  Cardiff Explosives Conspiracy Tri-
    als *40*
  Cardiff Five *86, 100*
    hate towards *123*
Carsley, Don *40, 191*
case papers
  archiving *57*
Castree, Ronald *82, 143, 148*

Catford Three *161*
CCTV *42*
Cellophane Man *83, 84, 89*
Chapman, Mr Justice *156*
character traits *116*
Chepstow Laboratory *47, 61*
Christie, John *161*
Chuter-Ede, James *161*
circumstantial evidence *185*
Clarke, Donna *42, 193*
closure *108*
clothing *84*
Coalition *147*
'cocktail hypothesis' *77*
Code for Crown Prosecutors *41*
coincidence *47, 62*
cold cases *57*
  58
Collins, Michael *192*
Collins, Mr Justice *163*
Combined DNA Index System
    (CODIS) *89*
community *70*
  respect and support *69*
condom
  unused condom *116*
Confait, Maxwell *154*
confession *xiv, 39*
  deathbed confession *182*
confessions *48, 125, 169*
confidence *xvi, 170*
  public confidence *33, 138*
confidentiality *71, 73, 116*
conspiracy
  conspiracy theories *73*

conspiracy to pervert the course of
justice *40*

control

lack of control *116*

loss of control *118*

controversy *30*

corroboration *99*

corruption *173*

courage *77*

Court of Appeal *xiv, 42, 139, 143, 153,
157, 163, 187*

Court of Criminal Appeal *185*

Coutts, Chris *110, 172*

Cover, Harold *184*

cowardice *123*

Cracker *113*

credibility *77*

crime

bestial crime *125*

crime analysis *57*

crime detection *93*

Crime Faculty *53*

crime prevention *93*

crime scene *153*

reinterpretation of *61*

reports from *95, 116*

Criminal Cases Review Commission
(CCRC) *40, 153, 163*

Criminal Justice Act 2003 *137*

criminal justice system (CJS) *29, 30, 36,
38, 59, 64, 67, 115, 126, 127*

cross-referencing *61*

Crown Prosecution Service (CPS) *41,
43, 110, 113, 155*

cruelty *142*

D

danger *140*

Daniels, Michael *173*

Dark, Dr. Colin *61, 90*

Darvell brothers (Paul and Wayne) *40,
191*

Davies, Edmund QC *186*

Davis, Mr Justice *142, 149*

Dean, Nicholas QC *173*

decency *109, 127*

deception *40, 115*

de Maid, Bernard *186*

detention

indefinite detention *114*

deterrence *36, 136*

diminished responsibility *115*

Director of Public Prosecutions *xvi,
158, 176*

disclosure *102, 103*

DNA *xx, 47, 48, 49, 57, 61, 83, 114, 141,
150*

alleles (bands) *90*

amplification *50, 51, 58*

degradation *48*

destruction of excess DNA *87*

DNA age *36, 38*

DNA analysis *48*

DNA profile *78, 81*

DNA screening

intelligence-led screening *90*

DNA sweep *94*

random sweep *63*

DNA-testing *72, 74, 81, 115, 124, 126,
153*

advances in *51*

new system *67*

SGM+ *52*

start of *47*

familial DNA *33, 62, 91, 94*

foreign DNA *75*

hit *61, 95*

mass screening *86*

mouth swab *98*

National DNA Database *33, 61, 62, 63,*
    87, 89, 90, 92, 120, 154

sample *126*

SGM+ *52, 82, 89*

documents

lost documents *173*

drugs *117, 118*

Dutfield, Joy *70*

E

electrostatic depression analysis (ESDA)
    57, 191

Elfer, David QC *77*

Elias, Gerard QC *190, 191*

Ely *119*

entrapment *115*

equality of arms *134*

European Convention on Human Rights
    (ECHR) *136*

European Court of Human Rights
    (ECtHR) *136*

Evans, Evan Rev. *39, 182*

Evans, Harold *162*

Evans, Timothy *160, 161, 163*

evidence *81, 153*

circumstantial evidence *100, 184*

flimsy evidence *41*

honest gathering of evidence *73*

interpretation of evidence *153*

scientific evidence *139, 189, 194*

execution *31, 39*

exhibits *57*

contamination, etc. *57*

review of *79*

exhumation *62, 90*

exit route *85*

Explosives Conspiracy Trial *190*

F

Federal Bureau of Investigation (FBI)
    45, 89

fibres *46*

fingerprints *46, 49, 57, 79*

Fisher, Sir Henry *158*

Floyd, Pauline *60*

forensic science *37, 43, 44, 46, 47, 49, 52,*
    53, 60, 75, 77, 79, 81, 110, 124, 132

advances in *57, 64, 67, 106*

Forensic Alliance *34, 82, 83, 92, 94*

forensic science laboratory *61*

Forensic Science Service (FSS) *82*

loss of monopoly *63*

Franklin, Douglas *160*

frenzy *45, 108*

Fryer, John *158*

Fulton, Sir Forrest *165*

G

Gafoor, Jeffrey *xx, 30, 86, 91, 97, 123, 135*
  Gafoor-effect *133*
Gallup, Angela *82, 84*
Garth Colliery *62*
Gass, Tehar *169, 184, 186*
Germany *120, 130*
Gillard, John Bryan *173*
Gill, Dr. Peter *47, 77*
Goddard, Lord Rayner *161*
Goldring, Mr Justice *147*
Goode, Winston *155*
gratification *142, 143*
Green Chain rapes *114*
Green, Sarah *177*
Greenwood, Peter *173*
Griffiths, Margaret *70, 71*
Grommek, Mark *172*
Guildford Four *xiii, xx*
guilt *158*
  "presumption of guilt" *157*
Gurnos Estate *193*

H

Hacking
  Hacking, Bill *67*
  Hacking Report/Review *68, 72, 73, 106*
    withheld *75*
hair *46*
Hall, Darren *40, 189*
Hallett, Heather (Dame/Lady Justice)
  63, 142

Hampshire Police *58*
Hampson, Mark *63, 142*
handcuffing to hot radiators
  40
handwriting *57*
hanging *39*
Harrington, Patrick QC *104, 106*
Heald, Sir Lionel QC *161*
hearsay *42*
hectoring *xiv, 189*
Her Majesty's pleasure *136*
Hewins, Annette *42, 193*
Hibberd, Sarah-Jane *193*
Hibberd, Shauna *193*
Hibberd, Shauna and Sarah-Jane *42*
Hicks, Stephen *173*
Hodgson, Sean *58, 150, 160*
Home Office *50, 61, 82*
Home Secretary *136, 158, 161, 181, 186*
honey-trap *113*
Hooper, Mr Justice *64, 147*
Horry, Frederick *182*
Hughes, Geraldine *60*
human contact *130*
  avoiding *105*
human rights *136*
  Human Rights Act 1998 *136*
Humphreys, Travers Christmas KC *161*
Hutton, Stuart *64*
hypotheses *47, 153*

I

identification

identification evidence *167*

misidentification *164*

informers *189*

injuries database *77*

innocence *38, 153, 172*

presumption of innocence *159*

insanity *128, 186*

Instituts für Rechtsmedizin at the University of Münster *83*

integrity *77, 110*

Interpol *89*

interview *40, 99, 133*

interview strategy *134*

no comment *103*

tape-recording *40, 159*

investigation *42, 45, 46, 47, 57, 75, 100, 124*

intelligence-led *86*

investigative integrity *73*

modern investigative techniques *85*

re-investigation *57*

J

James, Lizzie *113, 115*

Jeffreys, Alec *48*

Jenkins, Granville *169, 186*

Jenkins, Roy *158, 162*

Jennings, Paul *173*

John, Carly *193*

Jones, Diane *42, 193*

Jones, Jeffrey *192*

Jones, Jonathan *41, 74, 156, 192*

Judges' Rules *156*

judicial murder *32, 185*

judicial review *153, 163*

justice *59*

juveniles *136*

K

Kappen, Joseph *60, 62, 90, 95*

Kappen, Paul *62*

Karen Skipper Inquiry *75*

Kelleher, Sharon *40*

Kelly, Ian *48*

Kiszko, Stefan *82, 148*

Knight, Bernard *116*

knives *45, 119, 127*

L

Lace, David *58, 150*

Lancashire Police *67*

Lasham, Pauline *114*

Latham, Lord Justice *143*

Lattimore, Colin *39, 155*

Law Commission *135, 146*

Lawrence, Stephen *xiii*

Lawton, Lord Justice *185*

lawyers *43, 136, 144, 154, 158, 171, 174*

defence lawyers *94*

Lay Advisory Group (LAG) *69*

legal aid cuts *xxiii*

Leighton, Ronald *39, 155*

leniency *143, 151*

lessons *30*

Leveson Inquiry *xvi*

Lewis, Lewis *181*

Lewis, Richard (and see Dic Penderyn) *31, 38, 181*

Lewis, Stuart *40, 189*

life imprisonment *30, 136*

Liverpool Echo *123*

Llandarcy *60, 62, 90, 94*

   Llandarcy murders *33*

Llanharan *105*

loner *130*

Lord Chief Justice *136*

Lynette White Inquiry *43, 44, 47, 48, 52, 64, 67, 68, 74, 82, 116*

M

MacDonald, Andrew *91*

Macpherson Inquiry *xiii*

Maddison, Mr Justice *172*

Maguire Seven *xx*

Maid, Bernard de *64, 100, 103, 163*

Major Crimes Review Unit (MCRU) *65, 67, 75*

malpractice *xx, 158, 159*

manipulation *43, 49, 82, 189, 192*

Mann, Linda *48*

manslaughter *148*

Mant, Professor Keith *160*

Marwood, William *182*

Massey, Ian *173*

Mattan, Mahmood *31, 39, 184*

Maxwell Confait Inquiry *39*

Maxwell-Fyfe, Sir David *162, 186*

McCann, Patrick *42*

media *43, 73, 87, 110, 132*

Melbourne, Lord *181*

mental issues *117, 119, 131*

Merthyr Tydfil

   Gurnos Estate *42, 193*

   Merthyr Rising *181*

   Merthyr Two *87*

Metropolitan Police Service *xiii, 69*

Miller, Stephen *xiv, xvi, 30, 37, 87, 107, 120, 125, 189*

Mills, Norman *70*

Ministry of Justice *135, 146, 147, 150*

miscarriage of justice *xx, 29, 30, 37, 45, 53, 59, 81, 125, 147, 153, 157, 163, 172*

   gross miscarriage *111*

   preventing miscariages *93*

mistakes *39, 60*

mitigation *138, 140*

Molseed, Lesley *143*

motivation *45*

Mouncher, Graham *118, 173, 190*

murder *41, 45, 48, 58, 60, 74, 93, 115*

   murder manual *67, 68*

   savage *124*

Murray, John *173*

N

Napper, Robert *113, 133, 149*

National Crime and Operations Facility (NCOF) *33, 52, 61, 77, 81, 121, 134*

National Criminal Intelligence Service
    (NCIS) *113*
National Injuries Database (NIB) *81*
National Policing Improvement Agency
    (NPIA) *134*
Neath *61*
Newsagents Three *39, 64, 189, 190*
Newton, Sandra *60*
Nickell, Rachel *113, 115, 121, 149*
ninhydrin *48*
nondescript *128*

O

O'Brien, Michael *31, 104, 189*
O'Brien, Rachel *173*
offender background characteristics *134*
offender profiling *61, 113, 115, 121, 129,
    130*
    father of *116*
    run-of-the-mill profiles *132*
Ognall, Mr Justice *113, 115*
O'Neill, Kevin *72, 75, 98, 100, 110*
openness *67*
Openshaw, Mr Justice *143, 149*
Operation Magnum *33*
Operation Mistral *79, 85, 90, 98, 101,
    105, 132*
Operation Rubicon *110*
ordinariness *119, 128*
Ormerod, Mr Justice/Lord Justice *185*
Ormrod, Mr Justice/Lord Justice *158*
Outteridge, Ronald *82*

P

Page, Thomas *173*
paint *85, 101*
Palk, Geraldine *63, 142, 144*
panic *108*
paper trail *58*
pardon *162, 163*
Paris, Tony *30, 37, 87, 104, 109, 126, 171*
Parker, Ianto *32, 39, 182*
parole *35, 124, 135, 138*
    Parole Board *136*
Parry, Brent *75, 98, 100, 110*
Partridge, Alan *40*
pathology *61, 157, 158*
Pedder, Keith *113, 133*
Penderyn, Dic (and see Richard Lewis)
    181
people of interest *78, 86*
    tracing *78*
perjury *172, 189*
Perriam, Violet *173*
perverse verdict *185*
perverting the course of justice *172, 193*
Pesticcio, Peggy *38, 50*
Phillip Saunders Inquiry *40*
Phillips, Sandra *191*
Phillips, Sir Cyril *159*
Phillips, Wynne *63, 109*
Pierrepoint, Albert *183*
Pitchford, Christopher QC *41*
Pitchfork, Colin *47*
Plumstead Common *114*
police
    hostilities towards *76*

new dawn in policing *68*

open policing *71*

Police and Criminal Evidence Act 1984
  (PACE) *39, 155, 159, 189*

transition period *41*

Pooley, Paul *160*

Pope, John *142, 192*

pornography

Gafoor offended by *130*

Powell, Richard *173*

Power, Harry *169*

Preddie, Rickie and Danny *147*

premeditation *138*

Price, Christopher MP *157*

prosecution

Prosecution of Offences Act 1985 *43*

tests *43*

prostitutes *37, 101, 107, 108, 116, 118, 124,*
  128, 142

protocols *61, 106*

Psaila, Angela *47, 172*

psychiatric report *140*

psychology *57*

psychological profile *116*

public

public confidence *xvi*

public scrutiny *xvi*

public inquiry *31, 32, 38, 41, 43, 64, 109*

public opinion

court of public opinion *164*

Pugh, Wayne *173*

punters *81, 101, 116, 124, 131*

Q

quality control *134*

quiet

keeping quiet *145*

R

racism *xiv, 184, 185, 187*

rage *117*

Rand, Dr. Stephen *83*

rape *48, 58, 60, 63, 90, 93, 115*

reconstruction *78, 85*

records

computerised records *61*

red herrings *154*

Rees, John Charles QC *41, 45, 103, 127,*
  144, 193

relationships *117, 119*

coping with *119*

release *30, 35, 108, 115, 124*

remand *37, 148*

time spent on remand *142*

remorse *35, 36, 63, 107, 117, 123, 124, 125,*
  127

responsibility *126, 128, 141, 149*

retribution *136*

review

fresh-start review (Hacking Review) *61*

Rhys-Roberts, T *184*

risk to the public *136*

Roath *105*

Roberts, Ludon *169, 184*

Rogers, John QC *89, 103*

Rogers, Tony *32, 64, 67, 98, 110*

Rose, Lord Justice *187*

Ross, Malcolm *74*

Rougier, Mr Justice *41*

Royal Commission *157, 159*

　Royal Commission on Criminal Pro-
　　cedure *159*

Royce, Mr Justice *35, 104, 109, 135*

Rule of Law *157*

S

sadism *35, 37, 97, 106, 130, 135, 142, 192*

safeguards *88, 94*

Salih, Ahmet *39, 156*

samples *64*

　storage of *58*

Sandra Phillips Inquiry *44, 191*

Saunders, Phillip *40*

savagery *139*

Scarman, Lord Justice *158*

scene of crime *43, 45, 77*

　photographs *78, 83*

　scenes of crime officers *46*

science *153*

　forensic science *154, 155*

　scientific evidence *189, 194*

　　lack of *41*

Scott-Henderson, John QC *162*

scrutiny *xvi*

Seaford, John *173*

Second Generation Multiplex (SGM) *50*

Seligman, David *70*

Sellers, Mr Justice *161*

semen *63, 92, 101, 117*

　asperic semen *118*

serial killers *60*

serious crime *134*

　Serious Crime Analysis Section
　　(SCAS) *134*

sexual overtones *107, 116, 142*

shame *108*

shanking *124*

Sherwood, Ellis *189*

short-tandem-repeats (STR) *50*

silence *100*

Silverman, Sir Sydney MP *162*

Simone, Teresa di *58, 150*

Simpson, Keith *158*

Skewen *62*

Skipper, Karen *42, 142, 149, 192*

Skipper, Phillip *42, 149*

skirting board *84*

Skuse, Frank *82*

smear on communal door *83*

South Wales *xiii*

South Wales Police *30, 32, 38, 40, 50, 53,
　　64, 74, 83, 109, 128*

　Major Crimes Review Unit (MCRU)
　　32

　Professional Standards Department
　　32, 65

Splott *119*

stabbing *45, 97, 107, 114, 124, 143*

Stagg, Colin *113, 121, 149*

stakeholders *68, 100*

Starmer, Keir QC *176*

statute of limitations *31, 59, 183*

Stephen, Paul *173*

stereotypes *132*

stigma *32, 35, 38, 89, 97, 139, 141, 169, 187*

Stockwell, Graham *156*

storage

  materials of *57*

suffering *141*

suicide *58*

  attempted suicide *98, 126*

  Gafoor attempt *35*

Sullivan, Denise *42, 193*

surveillance *92, 94, 98, 99, 118*

suspects *61, 79, 86, 156*

  death of *62*

  prime suspect *118*

  viable suspects *47*

  vulnerable suspects *39*

Swansea *30*

  Swansea Crown Court *173*

Swanwick, Mr Justice *158*

Sweeney, Mr Justice *173*

systemic failure *xiii*

temper *45, 127, 130*

Thames Valley Police *40*

Thomas, Alun *192*

Thompson, Beverley *70*

Thornley, John *67*

time

  passage of time *57*

Tooze, Harry and Megan *41, 74*

Tottenham Three *xiii*

trainer-prints *46*

transparency *xvi, 68*

trauma *129*

trust *75, 87, 88, 94*

truth

  tendency to emerge *154*

U

uniqueness *128*

Usher, Alan *160*

T

tape-recording *xiv, 99, 103*

tariff *xvi*

tariffs *30, 35, 135, 137, 142*

  starting points *137*

  tariff system *36*

taxi drivers *124*

Taylor, Damilola *147*

Taylor, Lord *30, 40, 189, 192*

Teare, Donald *158*

tell-tale signs *128*

V

Venables v UK 137

"verbals" *39, 189*

victims *xx, 31, 32, 43, 49, 59, 64, 108, 109, 114, 128, 140, 148*

  victim impact statement *140*

  victims' families *62*

Vilday, Learnne *172*

vindication *xx, 29, 31, 111, 150, 151, 153, 169*

violence *39, 116, 117, 119, 128, 139*

sexually motivated *142*
    violent outbursts *118*
Volpert, Lily *184, 187*
vulnerability *39, 40*

Yorkshire Ripper *52*
Young, Julian *58*

W

Ward, Judith *xx, 82*
Webster, Mark *49, 50*
Welsh Nationalists *190*
West Midlands Crime Squad *xiii*
West Midlands Police *74*
whispering campaign *59, 92, 97, 114*
Whitaker, Dr. Jonathan *61, 90*
White, Lynette *xx, 30, 37, 59, 113, 118,*
    121, 135
Whiteside, Dr. John *47, 77, 172*
White, Terry *37, 97, 123*
Williams, John QC *172, 187*
Williams (Lord Williams of Mostyn) *190*
Williams, Paul *91, 94, 95, 98, 100, 106,*
    110, 132
Wimbledon Common *113*
witnesses *160*
    civilian witnesses *172*
Woledge, Peter *156*
wounds *139*
    wound analysis *77*

Y

Y-chromosome *82*
Yellen, Anthony *40*